NICE GIRLS
DO GET THE
SALE

RELATIONSHIP BUILDING
THAT GETS RESULTS

Elinor Stutz

SOURCEBOOKS, INC.®
NAPERVILLE, ILLINOIS

Published by Sourcebooks, Inc.
P.O. Box 4410, Naperville, Illinois 60567-4410
(630) 961-3900
Fax: (630) 961-2168
www.sourcebooks.com

Originally published in 2005 by Smooth Sale publishing

Library of Congress Cataloging-in-Publication Data
Stutz, Elinor.
  Nice girls DO get the sale : relationship building that gets results / Elinor Stutz.
    p. cm.
  Includes index.
  ISBN-13: 978-1-4022-0744-0
  ISBN-10: 1-4022-0744-1
  1. Selling. 2. Sales management. 3. Customer relations. I. Title.

HF5438.25.S78 2006
658.85--dc22

                                                          2006016346

          Printed and bound in the United States of America.
               VP 10 9 8 7 6 5 4 3 2 1

Contents

Acknowledgments

First and foremost, a huge thank you to my husband, who gave direction to my sales career throughout the years and who lent tremendous encouragement to my authoring a book.

Secondly, much love to my children, Jeff and Netanya. As teenagers, they motivated me not to give up on my sales career. Now in their adulthood, Jeff is always available to offer excellent advice on hardware and software issues, and when needed, he will cheerfully lend a helping hand.

Netanya, after hearing just one more sales story, suggested I write a book. In her mind, I was always easily able to find solutions, no matter the degree of difficulty of the sales situations. She thought my analytical and methodical processes were noteworthy and should be shared. Netanya thus named my sales training business, Smooth Sale.

Authoring a book is only a piece of the process. Getting the book to market with a professional flare for others to notice is the more difficult challenge. Sandra Yancey, CEO of eWomenNetwork, had the foresight to establish a new division, eWomenPublishingNetwork, in order to help and promote female authors.

A special thank you to Jan B. King, Editorial Director of eWomenPublishingNetwork and her associated publishing professionals who helped me put this book in your hands:

Gloria Balcom, The Next Level Marketing, Los Angeles, CA; and Linda Jay Geldens, Copyeditor, Kentfield, CA; and Nancy Cleary, Book Branding, Deadwood, OR; and Randy Peyser, AuthorOneStop, Aromas, CA, who presented this manuscript to Sourcebooks.

Foreword

The sales information compiled in this book is an accumulation of eleven years of corporate sales experience. Industries in which I participated and from which I draw real life sales experience include copiers, high-end networked printers and software, and online advertising.

I began my sales career as a ninety-day "trial" copier representative, having to walk the territory to find business.

Although I had no prior sales experience, knew nothing about the business equipment (copiers, shredders, and fax machines) I was supposed to sell, and my company offered no sales training, I rose to be the top producer in my sales organization within the fourth month of being hired. Up until the sixth month, it was a good ol' boys network. Not only was I the only woman on a team of five salespeople in the branch office, but there had never been a woman on the sales team before me. Across the country, the entire management staff was male. I was in solitary confinement, as no one would speak to me except for the female secretaries. I had definitely crossed over the line of what was an acceptable female office position. Consequently, I was left to my own devices to figure out the selling process.

I quickly realized men and women sell very differently. Generally speaking, one major difference is men will go for their prospect's jugular while women will go for their heart.

Salesmen view saleswomen as being weak, in that they care about being liked by each prospect, they nurture each account, and move slowly in the sales cycle to get to know the person behind the title. Saleswomen turn negative thoughts into positive strategies. Their method of ensuring they are liked is to pay attention to the smallest details and follow up promptly on requests while keeping their eye on the bigger picture. While this is a slower road to get started, ultimately women will earn larger sales and far more repeat business, referrals, and testimonials than their male counterparts.

My uniqueness catapulted me to the top of this sales organization. In spite of all the negativity toward me for simply being a woman, I was still able to go into the field every day, smile, and learn everything there was to learn about my clientele through relationship building. By the sixth month, the manager gave up the silent treatment as there was no doubt I was the star performer.

Gradually, I made the titles of Major Account Manager and Account Executive, dedicated to Fortune 100 and 500 companies located in the Greater San Francisco Bay Area, including Silicon Valley. The cities include Pleasanton, San Ramon, Livermore, Foster City, Menlo Park, Sunnyvale, Santa Clara, and San Jose. In fact, competitors quit their territory, because I took major accounts away from them.

Much of the information I want to convey here appears in story form for quick reading. This style also serves to better explain how and why sales techniques work and are fun for the reader. In particular, you will learn how to easily overcome resistance from potential customers, as well as achieve your goals (whether setting up an appointment or gaining the actual business). Each step of the sales cycle is demonstrated throughout this book by using true field examples.

As you read through the stories, strategies, and tips, it will become apparent that it is possible to sell with profit in any economy, even a downturn. My early stories demonstrate that with no experience but lots of perseverance and a Nice Girl philosophy, you will succeed.

One competitor told me I had been nicknamed "The Bulldozer" because I always started at one end of the territory and covered every single street to the other end, acquiring new clients all the while. What my competitors did not know is that many of my clients would actually hug me upon greeting me. Their belief was, "Finally a vendor gets it!"

My specialty was turning around "cold" accounts and transforming angry clients into happy clients. I made it very easy for clients to do business with me by delivering exceptional service.

When you are starting out in sales, numbers matter the most—how many cold calls, telephone calls, and appointments you can rack up in a day, a week, a month. The process becomes easier, with results in a far shorter sales cycle, once you know how and why certain tried-and-true tactics and strategies work.

There are no magic secrets contained in this book. In retrospect, to be a top producer requires diligent work every day, striving to understand what your prospect wants, and doing your best to match those needs. All the while, you must build trust and confidence in potential clients, and become a value-added resource in order to make your competition disappear.

To sell anything, one must always show appreciation with simple but powerful words—please and thank you. A handwritten note is a long-forgotten custom for most salespeople, so your prospect will greatly appreciate receiving one. Writing a thoughtful thank-you note will set you apart from your competition.

Most important of all, sell with integrity. By the time I landed my last corporate job, I felt I had finally "made it." The base salary was substantial and the type of service I was selling was very exciting. Cell phones were just beginning to connect to the Internet. At that time, there would be a three to five second delay while the cell phones were trying to send and receive to the Internet. I was selling advertising to appear during the lag time on these cell phones, as a pilot program.

The new concept of placing advertising on cell phones was so exciting to everyone that the top advertising agencies in the country were lined up to be amongst the first to try out the new service.

To my horror, after all the hard work of developing my own promotional materials, learning about the new technology and associated jargon, and finding the executives who wanted to be among the first to purchase advertising space on the new technology was done and promises to deliver the service by May 2001 were made, I found out that the service did not actually exist.

I had been misled in meetings to believe the advertising

service was well within the stated timeline. It quickly became clear that the person in charge of implementing the service was avoiding me. We were situated in cubicles and as soon as he heard me coming, he would duck out the door. One day, I altered my path and went around the cubicles in the other direction. I had this person cornered, and he could not look me in the eye. I knew then the service I had been selling most likely would never exist. I later learned it was termed "vaporware."

Although I was earning big money, when the realization that I was offering vaporware hit me, I resigned on the spot. It was professionally embarrassing. I wanted to distance myself from the company. When I called my prospects to tell them I was leaving, I suggested they take five minutes after we ended the telephone call to contemplate why I might quit such an exciting project. They thanked me profusely for giving them forewarning.

If one is unethical, even large cities soon become small towns, because everyone talks. You must maintain integrity in all of your business dealings, or one day you will have no one left to call upon.

In summary, creativity will get you in the door, analyzing where you are in the sales cycle will point you to the next step, and selling with integrity will bring you repeat business, testimonials, and referrals.

This formula will also provide you with a higher closing ratio and greater profit. It may also help you become the next top producer.

Realizing the wealth of experience and fun stories I had to share, my business, Smooth Sale, was born and grew into a sales training company through products and services specifically designed for entrepreneurs, network marketers, and beginning salespeople. My desire is to help others avoid the pitfalls I faced and to help them build their business quickly and easily. For more information about Smooth Sale and our many offerings, please visit www.smoothsale.net or call 1-800-704-1499 to tailor a program specific to your needs.

NOTE: Names have been changed "to protect the guilty!"

The Nice Girl Philosophy

- Novice saleswomen can earn business from large companies simply by showing respect, and a willingness to work on the behalf of each contact and the company as a whole. One of the easiest steps to differentiate yourself from your competitors is to follow up on time and be prepared to conduct business. Most salespeople let requests and preparation for appointments slide as both require too much work. Follow-up and professionalism are the basis for trust; demonstrating trust and integrity are the qualifiers for building relationships.
- The small business owner and salespeople in less familiar companies can take business away from their better-known competitors—it is not impossible.
- You can and, in fact, must sell with profit—no matter the state of the economy.
- To build strong client relationships, you must begin by selling from the prospect's view of the world, and continually demonstrate credibility and trust. Next, you must value-add sell; that is, overdeliver on your prospect's expectations all the way through the sales cycle to make the sale a win-win for all concerned. An example of a value-add sell would be to offer your resources to your prospects as appropriate. One client of mine sells ergonomic computer equipment. I suggested where he

might demo his equipment to garner interest. Additionally, I referred a purchasing manager of a sizable company to him when she stated that she had a need for his type of equipment. The two of them satisfied each other's business needs, and they were both very impressed by the fact that I volunteered to share my resources, which exceeded both of their expectations.

Author's Note: The following pages are filled with proven sales concepts, strategies, and tips. Of course, you should only adopt those that are genuinely compatible with your personality and style.

1
Conclude vs. Close

Closing is seen as the finality of a treacherous sales cycle and fulfills either high hopes or dreaded nightmares for many businesspeople. In their minds, this phase of the sale has become both a preoccupation and an insurmountable challenge.

For this reason, closing is discussed both at the beginning and at the end of this book because it is the most asked-for topic and concerns salespeople the most.

Let me assure you there is no mystery to closing. As long as you methodically value-add sell throughout the cycle, you will be able to ask for the business in the natural flow of conversation.

Why do most people fear closing, and why are they afraid to ask for the business?

The answer is fear of being told either:

"No."

or

"Get out and never darken my doorstep again."

In order to avoid either of these unpleasant scenarios, some salespeople do not ask for the business and therefore fail to meet their sales goals.

How do you ask for business without being "the bad girl"?

- You must stop thinking that if you ask for the business, you are "the bad girl."
- You are actually "the Nice Girl" if you meet the client's needs. They will view you, at the very least, as a team player.
- Your client will also view you as a credible, knowledgeable resource, and will thereby reward you with repeat business, testimonials, and referrals.

Let's preview the sales cycle for a moment. Throughout the sales process, you will:

- Learn about the prospect's business.
- Build trust.
- Become a value-added resource.
- Understand the prospect's corporate challenges and personal goals. In fact, over time, prospects and clients will confide their personal thoughts to you.
- Lay out an excellent plan to resolve issues and help move the prospect's company forward in your area of expertise.
- Motivate the prospect to become your client.
- Build repeat business, testimonials, and referrals.

How on earth can anyone think of themselves as "the bad girl" or as "too pushy" if they accomplish all of the above? You are definitely the Nice Girl.

Knowing you have been attentive to your prospect, have found a solution to their liking, and now understand that you are the Nice Girl, isn't it easy to ask a question such as,

"When would you like to get started?"

Some well-known sales trainers suggest you memorize 102 closes. However, this would suggest that there are only 102 possible scenarios you will run across.

You need to understand that each person has their own unique view of the world, which might depend on their business environment, personal circumstances, genetics, and upbringing. If you believe the variations are infinite, then you will toss your script out the window. Scripted sales are viewed by many as very manipulative. To make matters worse, scripted sales sound phony because they are not specific to the prospect.

Responses need to be genuine and appropriate. You must treat each prospect as a unique individual in a unique setting and tailor your response accordingly.

The mere word, "close" sends shivers up the spines of many sales and businesspeople. Fear once again gets in the way—the fear of rejection, being told "no."

As you end conversation with your prospect, do so as if you are talking with a friend; that is, in the style of a natural conclusion. "Conclude," according to the thesaurus, is a synonym for "close." You may find it easier to work with "concluding" than with "closing."

When I first began my sales career, I admittedly needed to send my suits to the cleaners after only one wearing as I would perspire more than normal due to extreme nervousness. In time, my nervousness disappeared as I gained confidence in my ability to sell.

As you advance through the sales cycle to the point where you are concluding a conversation, it means that information has been exchanged. Being ready to conclude the conversation signals that you, as a saleswoman, have come to realize what will solve the prospect's problem(s), and you have solution(s) to offer.

If the question and answer period of your initial meetings was executed correctly, your prospect will have told you exactly what they are looking for and how to present an acceptable package to them. As you learn to prepare and conduct the sales cycle properly, it will become very easy to ask:

> • *"Which package do you prefer?"*
> • *"When would you like to take possession?"*
> • *"All I need is a down payment of $95,000."*
> • *"Please authorize the paperwork here."*

Throughout *Nice Girls DO Get the Sale* you will find true sales stories from the field that demonstrate how to advance past the men, respond to objections, move the sales process forward, and value-add sell from the prospect's and client's points of view so that you will have a quick lesson in using your innate abilities as a saleswoman and learn relationship selling.

Now we will explore each step of the sales cycle and pinpoint how you can differentiate yourself from the competition and how to relationship sell for enhanced business satisfaction. As we progress through the sales cycle, we will once again visit "the close" to draw you to a better conclusion.

Nice Girl Sales Tips

1. Change your selling mindset to positive by way of helping prospects solve problems.
2. Successful selling is based upon integrity, developing trust, and building solid relationships.
3. Think of "closing" as "concluding"—a natural progression.

2
The Sales Personality: Do You Have What It Takes?

To begin a sales career or a business takes a lot of courage. To go into sales as a woman has its own particular challenges. In addition to offering value and promoting your own services, there are intangibles to be learned, such as human emotion, and ideas and words that motivate prospects to become clients.

Your work to uncover the intangibles is based upon your ability to read the prospect. Note when your prospect's face lights up, or when he or she frowns, what excites the prospect, or what makes his or her arms fold. Observe what it is that you are doing to motivate the prospect to move through the sales cycle.

Aside from your sales goals, you need to set personal goals for achieving the knowledge to become successful. The category of knowledge includes sales skills, knowledge of your own industry, your top competitors' business models, and your prospects' businesses and industries.

All of these goals take a great deal of time and you will feel as if you are moving backward instead of forward. In spite of setbacks, you must be prepared to persevere.

Another key to success is to politely acknowledge negative comments with a smile as a Nice Girl would, and then proceed more determined than ever. Most often, you will find the negativity stems from the other person's insecurity. They fear you will succeed where they could not. Your attitude is everything. Knowing the negative party is fearful of your intended success means they actually believe you will succeed. This is why you should smile upon hearing negative comments! Turn the negativity into motivation to propel yourself to success.

The copier industry in the 1990s was so difficult and competitive that office doors were continually revolving with new employees in and old employees out faster than you could count them. People just gave up, plain and simple. They weren't willing to work to get beyond the obstacles or to motivate themselves to get to the next level.

One of my favorite memories is from my first job. I kept a list of all the people who became employed by the company and quit within thirty days or less. A notable fact is every single one of these people were men. As I wrote their names on a yellow legal pad and drew a line through their name when they left, I wondered if other women would have left as quickly if they had been given the opportunity. These salespeople walked out and never said goodbye.

Of the core group of five salesmen, two quit by the end of the first year. The first salesman of the two that quit was focused on a highly specialized calculator whose market was rapidly shrinking. The second salesperson fell into the category of being fearful to ask for business. He enjoyed making friends with prospects but was fearful of helping to solve their problems and asking for their business. Three of us remained at the east Bay branch of the company.

A coworker, who had helped me recall some of the names listed on my yellow pad, was in the San Francisco office on the day I resigned. I faxed the list to him, with my name crossed out on the top. To my surprise and embarrassment, the director of sales happened to be standing at the fax machine at the exact moment the list was received.

He was not amused by the list, which was entitled "Company Hit List," but my colleague was figuratively rolling on the floor—and laughing uncontrollably.

My mantra is to always succeed. I would find it terribly embarrassing to fail at any step of the way. Failure is not in my vocabulary and is simply not an option for me. When I encounter difficult times, I step back from the situation and analyze where I am stuck, what the options are, and formulate how to proceed.

Believing in my ideas and my ability always got me through the tough times. In fact, I would like to publicly thank those individuals who rolled their eyes and had a smirk on their face when I told them what I was about to embark upon. And, thank you also to those who said:

> *"Too many people are already providing sales training, books, and CDs."*

and others who said:

> *"It's a myth you can make money on the Internet—don't believe it, and don't waste your time."*

Why, you ask, would I thank these individuals? I love a good challenge, and they presented me with a great one. Developing creative and untried methods to attain goals is part of the challenge and the competitive fun. Additionally, I find great satisfaction in proving I am right!

My Story

I spent fifteen years at home raising my two children. During the last eight years, I had a word processing business that I ran from home while the children were in school.

The income helped with everyday expenses, but was limited. There are only so many hours a day one can sit in a chair and type, and there was only a certain amount of money that could be charged per-hour for such a service.

My husband and I both knew that one day I would have to work full time. There was huge uncertainty as to my capabilities after having been home for fifteen years. One night, my husband came home and announced:

> *"I've got it. You have the personality of a salesperson!"*

With disbelief, upon hearing that announcement, I quietly asked:

> *"Is that a compliment or an insult?"*

My initial visualization of a salesperson was an unshaven, plaid jacket wearing, gum-chewing, used car salesman. At that time, the word "salesman" had an unsavory connotation.

Looking back, I now know it is true—I *do* have the personality of a salesperson and I changed my perception as to what that means!

As a salesperson, I'm intuitive about reading people. As a saleswoman, I care about what my clients tell me and strive to help them achieve their goals. Women, in general, have a greater need to be liked and strive to make certain everyone's needs are met. Saleswomen tend to go to greater lengths to ensure a client's happiness, including paying close attention to the details. While this entails more work, the end result is a thriving business stemming from repeat business, referrals, and testimonials. Most salesmen I have worked with do not understand this. They generally are in for the quick hit. Prospects sense this and buy from competitive vendors. This, in turn, accounts for the quick turnover of salesmen and their lack of success.

Care about others, and they, in turn, will provide a loyal following.

Ask yourself the following. Do you:
- Love a challenge?
- Have the determination to be right?
- Look for creative ways to find solutions?
- Persist in most matters?
- Not care when people tell you "No" or "You can't do it"?
- Fight for yourself?
- Like competition and gamesmanship?
- Enjoy finding solutions and helping people?
- Prefer a win-win scenario with clients?

• Enjoy being known for getting results in your office or field of expertise?

These are essential traits for a successful saleswoman.

3
Persevering against All Odds

Prelude to the First Sales Job

Now that I knew I had the personality of a salesperson, the rest was easy. The only thing I had to do was find a sales job. My husband's associates said:

> *"All she has to do is sell copiers for one year, successfully, and then everyone will want to hire her."*

In my naiveté, I bought a business suit and went on my first interview to sell copiers. Who wouldn't hire me? I was smart, well-dressed, and eager to learn and to sell.

The first two rounds at the very first company went extremely well. The manager liked me and told me that the last step was to oblige the director, Bob, by meeting with him.

Anticipating the pending offer, I walked in to Bob's office confidently, with a beaming smile. As he was reviewing my résumé, to my complete astonishment, Bob said to me,

> *"Your résumé is a crock of sh...!"*

I couldn't imagine anyone having the gall to say something like that in an interview. But then I understood—this was my first test, to see if I could handle an angry customer. How clever his technique was! So I responded:

> *"At first glance, you may think that, but then you will see I have accomplished XYZ and these were the results..."*

Bob, who was well over six feet tall, stood up at that point and bellowed at me in his loudest voice:

> *"I mean it; your résumé is a crock of sh..—Now get out of my office!"*

Have you stopped laughing?

What this director did not realize is, his vocabulary and body language both contribute to what I term, his "DNA."

What do I mean? Detectives use DNA samples to identify victims. Your vocabulary and your body language are unique to you. As other people become familiar with you, they will anticipate how you will react both verbally and physically. These attributes become identifiers of your unique personality—or in my definition, an adjunct of your DNA.

As a businessperson, it is an absolute must to listen to vocabulary and to watch body language when you are selling to a prospect or visiting with a client. (This will become evident as you read through the book.)

I immediately rose from the chair, shook my head, and on my way out muttered, *"One day I'll show you!"*

There was the challenge!

Nice Girl Sales Tips

1. If you think you can—very likely, you can!
2. Avoid those who say you can't.
3. Be open to new ideas.

Another Interview Test

After many calls to copier companies, none of whom wanted to hire a female salesperson, I found one director, Jack, who finally agreed to grant me the privilege of interviewing.

Six interviews were required of me in order to be able to sell an unknown brand of copiers door-to-door. The end result of the six interviews was that Jack told me:

> *"Everyone seems to like you."*

(He didn't expect that to occur.)

> *"If only I knew someone who knows you, and could vouch for you, then I would hire you."*

Not realizing it at the time, I gave the appropriate sales response.

I acknowledged Jack's stipulation for hiring me, repeated the stipulation, and then used a "tie-down" question—that is, I qualified what he was telling me and made him commit to his statement. Here is that response:

> *"You mean, if I ever come across someone you know well, and they provide you with a good recommendation of my capabilities, then you will hire me?"*

NOTE: My response had an incredulous tone!

His response was a resounding "*Yes*" since he believed that I would *never* come across a person we both knew, due to our worlds being so different. In his previous career, this director had been a well-known athlete and still traveled in those circles, while I lived in suburbia with my family.

Very good friends of ours were absorbed by my interviewing process and found the stories highly entertaining and a source of great amusement. They knew of no one else who would have put up with all of this nonsense. I now had this new story with which to entertain them.

Only this time, an amazing coincidence happened. When Jack retired from sports, prior to joining the business equipment world, I learned he had tried his hand at being a stockbroker. The person he had reported to at that time was none other than my friend's father.

I had the sales director cornered!

The very next morning, with excitement and confidence in my voice, I called Jack and said:

> *"Do you remember telling me that if I met someone you knew and trusted, you would hire me?"*
> *"Yes,"* he said, hesitatingly.
> *"Well, do you remember Mr. John Smith? My husband and I are best friends with his son."*

Taking a deep breath, I asked:

> *"Will 8:00 Monday morning work for you?"*

....
Never be afraid to conclude business!
....

> *"Yes," he said with an audible sigh.*

I was so excited to have a job, and was laughing at the fact I had beaten Jack at his own game.

The next hurdle—and the most difficult—was working with the sales manager.

Moe

Moe was angry I had been hired. He had never worked with a woman before (this was September 1991) and told the other four salesmen not to talk to me and "maybe I would go away."

Talk about facing challenges! I had been at home for fifteen years, knew nothing about current business equipment (I was amazed that copiers were making automatic double sided copies), certainly knew nothing about sales, and there was no sales training to guide me. On top of all that, no one in the office was talking to me. I felt as if I were in solitary confinement.

People always ask, *"Why didn't you quit?"*

My feeling was that if I went elsewhere, I would have to start all over again, beginning with day one. By remaining at this office and overcoming the obstacles, I was at least advancing toward the goal of selling copiers for one year in order to do something else.

> *"Never give up on achieving your set goals."*
> —Elinor Stutz

I was set up. Everyone expected me to fail.

The only training I received was from the lead secretary, Lisa. My third morning, in the office, I whispered to her:

> *"How do I go about making sales?"*

Literally, no one was talking to me except for the secretaries, all of whom were female. Lisa's response was:

> *"I think you knock on every door in your territory."*

Wow, that was the key! I now knew everything there was to know about how to do my job, and I was going to be the best!

While the office was waiting for me to fail, I was planning to succeed.

What great advice I was given. I was eager to get started.

I truly knocked on every single business door in all three cities of my territory. The process became known as my marketing research. I learned that liquor stores and doughnut shops are very unlikely to use copiers. I also found out that small businesses did not and still do not have a lot of money to spend on options that increase the size of a sale.

It became clear, during the process, that my focus should be on medium- to large-sized companies. Once inside the larger companies, not only would there be greater potential for business, but also for repeat business.

> Repeat business, testimonials, and referrals are the key to sales success.

Meanwhile, back at the office, I was met with dead silence every afternoon. The men would tell each other jokes, slap each other on the back, and have a good old time talking it up big on what they had accomplished in the field that day. They just looked at me and wondered why I was still there.

From my point of view, it was good news/bad news that Moe wasn't speaking to me. He once bragged:

> *"My training in sales comes from selling vacuum cleaners door-to-door."*

He proudly added:

> *"To get in the house, I would 'accidentally' sprinkle dirt on the floor as the door opened a crack. Then I would offer to vacuum the mess for the little lady of the house."*

Upon hearing this story, I was extremely concerned. The phrase, little lady, sent shivers up my spine. Moe was the very last person from whom I would want to take lessons in selling. My desire was to become a *professional* saleswoman in every sense of the word. I wanted to be able to help my clients in such a manner that they would seek me out for advice and for repeat business.

Knowing the history of the manager gave me great willpower to stay away from him and succeed on my own!

Doing my best to ignore the male camaraderie and laughter, I deliberately walked straight to my desk each day to make more phone calls. Every afternoon I made at least twenty new phone calls, and every morning I made twenty follow-up phone calls. (This was before the introduction of email and the Internet.)

By 9:30 a.m. I would leave for the territory to make an average of fifty cold calls. At 3:00 p.m., I would head back to the office to avoid rush hour. I figured it was better to make more phone calls than waste time sitting in traffic.

- I made efficient use of my time.
- My day was systematized for maximum production.
- I always worked toward my set goals.

"Plan your work and work your plan!"
—Common sales quote and solid advice

After a few weeks, one young salesman took a liking to me and was quite nice to commiserate with. In fact, we still keep in touch. Recently, we exchanged stories of that first year. It turns out that on at least one occasion, we each had pulled off to the side of the road to cry from sheer frustration!

The others gradually following suit, began talking with me, and a true sales team began to develop. On occasion we even had fun together.

There was only one form of communication between myself and Moe, however. On a weekly basis, he would hand me a note stating that I was about to be fired. Mostly I ignored the notes. I alternated between feeling terror and shame, and I also experienced an amazingly strong desire to prove him wrong, fueled by extreme indignation.

However, on the fifty-eighth day, his note read:

> *"You have not sold one item yet. You have no prospects at hand. If nothing is sold within the next two days, you will be fired."*

This note had more intensity to it than the others. I believed I was close to a sale. So with anger that had built up from the past two months, I marched into Jack's office and asked:

> *"What is the meaning of this note? Our agreement was ninety days and I am holding you to it. And by the way, if I do not sell anything by that time, you will not have the pleasure of firing me. I will quit!"*

Anger got the better of me on that day. On the way out of the office, I slammed his door so hard, I was surprised the wall didn't cave in. Secretly, I think Jack admired my spunk. But, I was actually embarrassed by my behavior.

Miraculously, I was right about a sale being just around

the corner! On my eighty-ninth day, I sold a little calculator. Whew—I could keep my wonderful job. That one sale motivated me to make more phone calls and cold calls in my territory.

You might wonder, how did this scenario go from being the "Nightmare on Elm Street" to a wonderful job? That first sale made me realize that I was on to something good. Although I was approaching my territory and prospects in a different manner from everyone else, I was true to myself and it was about to pay off. I just needed more practice and consistency.

The sweet taste of success spurred me onward. I was making large numbers of prospecting cold calls to offices each day as well as phone calls. Every evening, I wrote thank-you notes to each person who helped me.

At the four-month mark, I proudly became the top producer in the office. Moe was furious with the men. He asked each of them:

> *"How can you let a female beat you?!"*

By the middle of the fifth month, Moe realized I was going to be the top producer once again. So he called all the men together and announced a contest for the end of the month—and this is what he said, verbatim (I'll never forget):

> *"If Elinor makes her numbers again, I'll treat you guys to a lingerie fashion show."*

Anger was a common theme to me in that copier sales office. I immediately asked:

> *"Since we're talking about my numbers, why don't we go to lunch, have a picnic, or even go to a ballgame?"*
>
> *"No" he said, "I promised the guys a lingerie fashion show and that's what we are going to do."*

For the next two weeks there was very little chatter in our office. The air was tense. I did not know what I was going to do about the reward for my sales numbers.

I pictured the venue for the fashion show, and thought, "sleaze." The show was going to be held at a restaurant attached to a motel, next to the freeway, on the wrong side of town.

To make matters worse, the models were a mother/daughter combo, and they would do private modeling of outfits for men interested in "purchasing" after the show.

The secretaries in my office were on edge, wondering what I would do if I once again brought in the most revenue, but they were afraid to ask. The end of the month came and I exceeded my numbers. Once again, I was the top producer.

The very next day, Moe announced:

> *"Okay, Elinor made her numbers. Which of you guys are coming to the lingerie fashion show?"*

That did it!

Furious, I once again found myself immediately standing in front of Moe's desk. As I banged my fist on his desk, I said in a very loud voice:

> *"Count me in!"*
> *"You can't come," he replied.*
> *"It's my number you are talking about," I shouted.*
> *"I don't care. You can't come," he retorted.*
> *"I'll tell you what," I said, absolutely livid by now,*
> *"Don't count me in, but you will be a chair short!"*

I stomped off to my desk to gather my belongings, glared at Moe one last time, and then left to go into the field.

Never make phone calls when you are sad or angry.

Meanwhile, Moe's face grew beet-red. He was feeling threatened that I might actually show. Even with the threat in place, I still didn't know what to do and the secretaries were still afraid to ask.

My car knew what to do. Somehow, at noon that day, I found myself in the parking lot of the location where the "fashion show" was to be held. Muttering under my breath, I walked in. I spotted the group, and, to their astonishment, I sat down.

Lunch was served, and the lingerie fashion show began. In those days, I was quite shy and never talked much in groups. Not that day! With purpose, I talked incessantly.

As the models neared us, I would call out across and down the table to the management figureheads to ask questions about how copiers worked. I asked directions to different cities. I did everything imaginable to take their attention away from the models and keep my coworkers on edge.

One salesman, sitting next to me, had the nerve to ask:

> *"I bet you don't wear anything like these outfits to bed. I bet you wear flannel, don't you?"*

Without skipping a beat, I retorted:

> *"I'll be glad to answer that question. But first, tell me, do you wear tops, bottoms, or nothing at all when you go to bed?"*

Needless to say, the first question was left unanswered.

Meanwhile, as the group was not allowed to enjoy the show, Moe called out to ask:

> *"Elinor, do you play poker?"*
> *"Yes," was my reply. I then added, "And I always win!"*

By the time I returned to the office (I had taken my time in order to cool off), the secretaries had heard the gossip and greeted me with high fives. I was their heroine. It felt good after all I had been through.

The next month, the salesman who had asked me about my nighttime attire asked one more question.

> *"How is it you know less about the equipment than any of us, have no prior sales experience, yet you outsell us each month?"*

He almost hinted that I was bribing clients. My response was:

> *"I do one thing none of you do. I'm actually nice to my clients!"*

While that may seem mean, it was the truth. I used to shudder when I heard my associates speaking about their clients and proudly bragging about how they were ripping them off.

When you are selling, your prospect senses you as would a sniffing dog. They know when you only have commission on your mind or when you are genuinely there to provide a win-win solution for all concerned.

> Always position yourself as a value-added resource and you will win more business.

By my sixth month there, everyone in the office was talking to me. Jack, the district manager, began to point to me as a perfect example of how to sell. He would tell everyone:

> *"Even when you become a seasoned sales rep, you must always do the basics (new calls and follow-up calls) to succeed, just like Elinor."*

However, I still had my ups and downs with Moe.

One other saga took place that is meaningful if you are trying to get into new accounts.

We had weekly Monday morning meetings at the ungodly hour of 7:30 a.m. This particular Monday, it was decided that to attract new clients, we needed to send out letters to everyone in our territory.

Even back then, I realized no one would want to read a three-page letter about copiers. Would you?

If the only sales tactic you ever use is to ask yourself, *"If I were the prospect, would I want to hear or receive **that**?"* you will know if you are on the right track.

However, the men in the office decided to send a three-page letter to our prospects describing all of the wonderful features of the copier and the expertise of the manufacturer in minute detail.

I tried my best to explain that no one would want to read such a letter. Moe held the following vote by demanding:

> *"Men, how do you vote? Are you with me?"*

I was voted down. The next step was to address the envelopes that evening at home. We were to bring everything back into the office the next morning.

The next day, I proudly handed my sealed envelopes to Moe. He was very upset and yelled at me:

> *"You were supposed to stuff the envelopes in the office this morning. We were all going to do it together."*

Slyly, I replied:

> *"Oh, I always hear you say that we should do paperwork at night and save the daylight hours for calling on prospects. So I sealed the envelopes last night."*

Steam was coming out of Moe's ears. I had unwittingly used an excellent sales technique. He could not refute his own words.

....
When working with a prospect and management, take note of their words on key points. Memorize the words or write them down in case they become a point of contention later on.
....

I left the office for my territory, while the men lagged behind, trying to get their envelopes sealed and ready for mailing. At the end of the day, we each put our one hundred letters in the mail and waited.

Very gradually, the phone began to ring—but only for me! By the end of two weeks, the four men received a grand total of zero phone calls and I, mysteriously, received six phone calls.

Finally, Moe looked at me and said:

"Okay, it's time to come clean, what did you do?"

I reminded him that no one wanted to listen to me when I predicted that our prospects would not want to read a long letter describing the intricacies of copiers.

Knowing this, the night before the meeting, I went to the card shop and purchased a box of note cards. Each card pictured two beach chairs and a sun umbrella on a sandy beach near the ocean.

Inside the note card I wrote:

> *"Be carefree this summer. I will look after your equipment while you enjoy the beach and relax. Please call me at XYZ company for an appointment."*

My mailing was novel, fun, and it showed that I was truly thinking of the prospect. That's why I received the six calls. From then on, I always sent unique mailings, and they always succeeded in getting me in the door of desired accounts.

- Adapt sales training techniques to your style.
- Be true to yourself and your clients/prospects.
- Do not use advice that does not work for you.
- Always begin from the prospect's point of view.

Nice Girl Sales Tips

1. Believe in yourself.
2. Fight for yourself.
3. Do not let others influence you to give up.
4. Devise your plan.
5. Always work your plan.
6. Perform the basics every day—make calls and follow up.
7. Do not memorize scripts.
8. Listen well to each individual.
9. Sell in real time.
10. Accept challenges.
11. Keep refining methods until you find perfection.
12. Strive to win and enjoy winning.
13. Seek alternative ways to get your point across.

14. Keep asking questions in order to learn.
15. Be persistent.
16. Sell to others the way you would like to be sold to.
17. Market yourself differently from everyone else.
18. Face your obstacles one by one to overcome them.

4

How to Defeat the Best-Known Vendor While Still an Amateur *and* Selling an Unknown Brand

While striving to learn how to sell to larger companies, during my first year I came upon a well-known business in my territory. This company was in the process of beginning to build cell phone units.

Cell phones were not in existence yet, and I had absolutely no idea what the people at this company were talking about. However, it was very apparent that they were under the gun to get their technology up and running.

I kept making visits to the site, meeting with lower-level personnel. They always treated me cordially and we began to develop friendships. Gradually I was introduced to others within the department.

I became comfortable asking them questions about their business so that I could truly understand it. Again, this was prior to the Internet. We also began to talk about our families, hopes, and desires.

By the fourth meeting, they let me know that the company was moving to a larger, more modern facility. This was the opening I needed to find out about plans for additional equipment. I mustered up the courage to ask about their business equipment situation. As trust developed, the truth came out that they were less than happy with their current, well-known vendor.

I asked who made the decisions for the equipment and was directed to a very nice woman, Linda. She was frazzled by all of the duties she was saddled with. Linda truly did not want to take the time to talk about copiers, particularly an unknown brand. It was unthinkable that the company would switch from the best-known vendor to an unknown. But being the polite person she was, Linda invited me to her office and we talked.

We immediately developed a liking for one another. I sensed that we could talk more freely off-site, so I offered to take Linda and the people who referred me to her out to lunch.

At lunch, we all got to talking about family life, the weekend, and gradually the pros and cons of work. The sales cycle began to move forward at this luncheon. The inside gossip about their office slowly leaked out.

I was now at a "trusted friend" level.

It became clear:

• That they were unhappy with the machines being down,
• That the representative of the vendor company disappeared when was there was a problem, and
• That the vendor only wanted to sell new equipment and collect additional commission dollars.

Many meetings took place and I got to know each of the players personally. After every meeting, I sent a thank-you note for their time to each person in attendance. On occasion,

I would send a clever postcard to make the message more interesting.

They were among the prospects who received and loved the beach postcard. I was told it was their favorite.

When they read, *"Occasionally a copier may go down, but as your representative, I will always take care of you,"* they found the message poignant. It was a very important "value-add" for them, particularly since their current vendor could care less.

At one point, I learned that Linda loved sports. To her delight, I brought my director (Jack, the former athlete) to meet her, and she appreciated my thoughtfulness. Not knowing what to do about making an equipment decision, Linda said I had to meet her boss because he was the one to sign off on agreements.

Linda was trying to push off the decision to buy on to her boss. (While Linda wanted me for their new vendor, she did not want to be the person in charge of making that decision. There was always the possibility something major could go wrong and choosing me could be what was known as a "career bender.")

Being a novice, I did not realize Linda was confident that I would not be able to get an appointment with her manager, Carl. Among Carl's duties were the finances of the company.

Carl absolutely did *not* want to meet with me. He said:

"Everything is fine."

I countered:

> *"Even with the machines being down and lack of vendor response?"*

First hand knowledge is the best ammunition.

He then said:

> *"I'm too busy."*

I asked my favorite question:

> *"Do you ever eat?"*

Carl laughed and chided me:

> *"Of course I eat."*

My reply was:

> *"Then if you like, for thirty minutes of your time, I will bring lunch in. We will eat at your desk, and, at the same time, discuss changing your business equipment for something that works."*

I had made an offer he could not refuse.

Time was a major issue but not the only one. Carl was tired of hearing nonstop complaints about the equipment and the lack of caring on the part of the vendor. On the other hand, he was not about to share this last fact with me.

Carl only voiced an objection to the time factor involved. Going out for lunch takes a minimum of an hour. Talking business takes another thirty minutes to an hour.

I only asked for thirty minutes, which easily saved him one hour. In addition, he would receive lunch at no cost.

I had Carl in a corner. I met every one of his objections with a smile and with solid knowledge. The inside gossip was the incumbent male vendor had inadvertently caused company teams to be formed, fighting over the merit of securing a new vendor vs. remaining with him and his well-known products. I was baffled as to why he would have done this. In my mind, it certainly did not help his cause. With all of the unrest in the office, Carl owed it to the company to hear me out. He had nowhere to go but to say, "Yes."

We did meet. I brought the gourmet sandwiches as promised. I also met with Carl's wholehearted approval.

I saved him both time and money—key ingredients for making a sale.

Or, in this case, for advancing the sale.

Carl sent me back to speak to Linda, with these final words:

> *"The equipment is in Linda's department and so it is her decision to make."*

Feeling like a yo-yo, I knew that the decision to go with my company was back in her hands again. This time I was told:

> *"I want you and your husband to meet my husband and me at our home on Saturday afternoon."*

This request put a burden on our family as the trip was quite far—forty-five miles one way, across a bridge, and up a winding hill. But seizing the opportunity, I said *"Sure."*

A lot was riding on this sale. It was the largest company, to date, that our sales team had entertained. I was competing against the largest, best-known vendor. And, I was trying to sell our newest, largest, fastest piece of equipment that had just been released for us.

If I was successful, not only would I meet an accelerator for meeting and exceeding quota, I would make the quarterly bonus as well as a huge add-on bonus. I would now become the top producer of several branches.

I couldn't be certain if the salesmen in my office were for me or against me as the manager kept asking, *"How can you let a female beat you?"* Occasionally, regional management would walk into the office, speak to a couple of the men, and totally ignore me. Given the reaction of management toward me, I was doubtful there were saleswomen on the other company sales teams. I therefore viewed this sale of utmost importance. Once the sale was complete, I would become a force that management could no longer ignore.

Linda was very afraid to make the decision about switching brands of equipment from known to unknown. She acted as if her job were on the line. One bad move and she would be fired. It was evident that her husband was more experienced in business and could more easily discern if I were trustworthy. In fact, Linda just about told me so.

The question came down to *trust*. Would my husband and I come across as upright citizens who could be trusted, and could I be counted on to take care of Linda's company if problems were to arise with the equipment? The visit was to size my husband and me up to determine if we were worthy of this monumental decision. (My belief is my husband added one more testament to my "character" and whether or not I could be trusted.)

When a behavior strikes me as strange, such as extending this invitation to my husband, I try to understand where it stems from. Linda was under great pressure from her male management. At that time, we were all conditioned to purchase from men. I was an anomaly and clearly she was afraid to make a decision in my favor. Given she was insecure in this position, she looked to her husband to help her out because she viewed him as being more business savvy. The fact that we two women were fairly new to business became magnified. Linda must have believed the men would relate well one-on-one and during conversation her husband would extract a secret or two about my ability or inability from my husband. Subsequently, we two businesswomen became inconsequential. It was the men now doing the selling and making the decision.

Sometimes you have to bite your lip and play by the client's rules if you want to secure a win. I was not happy deferring to our husbands after all of the hours of hard work invested in this account. However, I was and still am proud I have a husband who will always support me, and I could almost taste the victory.

Unknown to Linda, I was under a deadline to seal the contract by 5:00 p.m. that Saturday in order to earn a hefty bonus. Our meeting in her home was at 3:00 p.m. I had been given a key to my office to enable the faxing of the paperwork to our home office by the deadline, if the contract were authorized.

> **NOTE:** I never ever mentioned bonuses and deadlines to any prospect or client, because if I were in their shoes, I would find that offensive. This is just one more example of how I differentiated myself from the male competition.

Because Linda had her own contract that we had to sign (that was a switch from the norm), I had no idea how I would make the deadline since the appointment took place at her home, which was far away from our respective offices.

Uncertain and inexperienced about how to advance the sale and close within the guidelines, I went the route of being as gracious as I knew how. As a gesture of thanks for being invited to their home, I brought a homemade banana bread.

I knew little about sales or the equipment, so I was always extra kind to prospects and clients. I made certain to always treat them in the same manner as I treated guests in my home.

> Prospects and clients should always be treated with great interest and respect.

Linda and her husband were delighted that I brought the bread. We sat and talked about hobbies, travel, and other interests. I never once mentioned the equipment that I so desperately wanted to sell.

The banana bread put us to goal. Linda and her husband were amazed that I went the extra mile to bring a gift after having been asked to give up a Saturday afternoon. My husband and I passed the test with flying colors!

To my great surprise and relief, the paperwork was waiting on her kitchen counter. Linda authorized the contract in my presence.

On the way home, we stopped at the office to fax the paperwork to the East. We made the 5:00 p.m. deadline by about a minute, and I was ecstatic!

With the bonus, I treated my family to see the stage show, *Phantom of the Opera*. Basking in my glory for having sold a very large system against the best known competitor to a Fortune 500 company, and within the set deadline, I had a sudden awakening. I was horrified the following Monday morning to hear that management decided I wasn't entitled to the hard-earned bonuses. Their reasoning was, since they did not have the equipment on hand at the time of the order, I did not qualify under the deadline.

Be aware that Nice Girls on occasion have to fight back not with fists but with thought and everything within their means. I countered that the deadline was set for the paperwork; availability of the equipment was not my problem but theirs. They were obviously angry that a female was the first salesperson to sell this new, large system and win all the bonus money and all company recognition. The extra earnings were never sent.

I was seething with anger. I decided to match my opponents. I had met Mary, a twenty-two-year-old, beautiful, blue-eyed blonde, who wiggled while she walked. I asked Mary to serve papers to Jack, the director of sales. She took delight in the devious act. Mary told me she loved the "quirky people" out in California compared to the more traditional people in Michigan from where she hailed. Mary phoned Jack for an interview appointment. The sixty-year-old director lit up and postured when he saw Mary walking toward him. They talked and flirted for a while and then he asked for her résumé. She pulled the papers out of her pocket and whispered in her sexy voice, "Consider yourself served." Mary then quickly ran out of the office.

When the court date arrived, Jack greeted me, but I was still angry and it was difficult to be cordial. Jack was a tall, suave, and handsome man. He had considerable speaking experience, a deep convincing voice, and gave an excellent account of what previously happened in his terms. I was certain the case was all over. But my father had taught me to play each game to the final end because frequently there will be a surprise ending.

The judge called me before him to tell my side of the story. I began my story of how I sold an "Agile" copier system against Brand X.

The judge stopped me mid-sentence and asked, *"What is an Agile?"* I explained it was a Japanese make of copier not too well-known. The judge stopped me cold. To my surprise, I heard him say, "I've heard enough. If you can sell an Agile copier against Brand X to any company, let alone a Fortune 500, you must be some fantastic saleswoman! If I had a sales team, you would be my Vice President!" The judge looked directly at Jack and said, "You pay her the bonus money that is rightfully hers." Bang went the gavel. Now, I was truly in my glory!

Reward yourself for success.

Sales Strategies Learned
Overcoming Objections
- Smile. An objection means people are listening to you and giving serious consideration to what you are saying.
- Make certain you understand the reasons for the objection—ask if you don't know.
- If a word is being used in a different manner than you are accustomed to, ask for clarification.
- If you do not understand something—ask. The client appreciates your sincerity of wanting to understand.
- Always put yourself in your prospect's/client's shoes and understand their challenges.
- Only then will you be able to devise an appropriate solution.
- Repeat the objection verbatim—using the other person's

vocabulary. The reason for this tactic is that if you find a solution for the objection and repeat back the original objection in their words, they cannot refute what they said.

"If I only knew someone who knows you and would provide a good recommendation, I would hire you."

The person was found and I had to be hired.

"I'm too busy to meet with you."

By offering to bring in sandwiches for the financial manager, I added an hour to the day. Taking it a step further, I only asked for thirty minutes—giving him a thirty-minute bonus. I found a solution and used his exact words to satisfy the objection.

Knowledge is power.

Always ask questions to learn more. Admit what you don't know. Promise to get the information on a timely basis. If necessary, bring in an expert. While this last step may extend the time involved in the process of selling, it will lend more credibility to you and your company.

- Since there was no training, I asked the secretary how to do my job.
- Internet research did not exist yet, so I asked all the contacts within the account questions about their business and goals.
- Buyers are more sophisticated today and *are* overwhelmed with work. Familiarize yourself with as much as you can about the company ahead of time.

- Study the prospect's mission statement, corporate officers, earnings, stock price, challenges, goals, key words, and top two competitors.

Nice Girl Sales Tips

1. Keep blinders on in regard to negativity.
2. Hear exactly what the objection is.
3. Repeat back the objection exactly as you heard it.
4. Clarify the objection if you do not understand all of the ramifications.
5. Ask the prospect what they believe will resolve the objection.
6. Repeat back the resolution exactly as you hear it.
7. Come to an agreement.
8. Live up to the action items of the agreement.
9. Put sales on hold until all is resolved.
10. Challenge yourself to keep learning.
11. Learn as much as you can about your own industry.
12. Familiarize yourself with your own top two competitors. These are not necessarily your biggest competitors but the ones you come up against most frequently.
13. Understand your competitors' Achilles heel and emphasize to your client where appropriate.
14. Do not bad-mouth your competition.
15. Know the similarities, but sell the differences.
16. Become the expert.
17. Share information freely.
18. Begin selling by standing in your prospect's shoes.
19. Become familiar with your prospect's industry.
20. Familiarize yourself with the prospect's website.

21. Look for repeated vocabulary (key words) on the website.
22. Key words reveal what is of utmost importance to the company.
23. Ask additional questions for further understanding.
24. Know your prospect's two top competitors to gain a handle on their industry and their business.
25. Learn your prospect's personal goals and corporate challenges.
26. Agility in understanding the two sides of each issue (yours and theirs) is essential.
27. Weigh what you offer against your prospect's mindset.
28. Develop a solution that will be mutually beneficial.
29. In larger companies, keep everyone in the loop in regard to developments. Read *Strategic Selling* by Stephen E. Heiman, published originally in 1998 by Warner Books.
30. Show attentiveness and genuine interest.
31. Back your statements with facts only.
32. Treat everyone with respect, equal importance, and always say "thank you."
33. Be as helpful as possible.
34. Free food always works for appointments, demos, and delivery of services.
35. The cost of the food has to be justified by the reward of the sale.
36. Do your best to understand each decision maker's point of view in one account.
37. Through questioning, find ways to save your prospect time and money.
38. Sell with integrity.
39. Analyze tactics for whether they will work.

40. Analyze where you may be stuck.
41. Be flexible to change course as needed.
42. Challenge yourself to try a new tactic.
43. Keep asking questions.
44. Play each game to the end.
45. Strive to do the best for your clients and it will be appreciated.
46. Thank-you notes go a long way.
47. Reward yourself for reaching difficult goals.

For the next eleven months, I was the top producer in two branches and won many awards. One quarter, I was honored for becoming the top producer for the western region. Yes, the manager, Moe, came to terms with my staying for a total of fifteen months. The director, Jack, had become proud of his "best" hire.

My first job in sales, as that of many other people, was solely a "numbers game." Just by the sheer volume of cold calls, walking the territory, and following up, one was bound to make a go of it, if not be successful. But I wanted more.

Although I was continually the top producer, won awards, and easily took business away from the competition during those fifteen months, I still felt as if I were in a dark closet trying to figure my way out.

My understanding and knowledge of how to advance the sales cycle was lacking. While it appeared that prospects liked me, I did not know why. I could not tell you why a prospect would become my client. Training became of utmost importance to me.

I was now ready for the next challenge.

5

Two Vital Keys to Success

Key #1: Passion

At two recent conferences, I had the thrill of hearing personal stories of female entrepreneurs who had started out with very little. One woman began with only a $25 box of business cards. With hard work, intelligence, and dedication these women built multimillion dollar companies.

None of these entrepreneurs had anything remarkable in their background, only courage. In fact, a few of the speakers had limited education. Others had been in abusive relationships years prior and had to overcome their sense of low self-esteem.

Every single one of these speakers said the secret to success is being passionate about what you offer and loving what you do.

> They did not give up on their dreams.

Once they found their passion, their attitude changed from, *"What do I **have** to do today?"* to *"What do I **get** to do today?"*

The other piece of advice they shared was, once you know your passion and what you plan to do, write out a business plan for a clear vision and full steam ahead.

I used to think, I'm a salesperson. I know I need business and I know how to get it. There is no need for me to write a business plan. But once I began to write my own plan, ideas crystallized and enhancements of what I had in mind for a future business immediately came to me.

> I captured all of my ideas in writing.

There would be no "forgetting." Now that I had a clear formula for success I wouldn't deviate from it but would pursue it. You may find the same idea will hold true for you.

Accept all invitations and opportunities that come your way. You may never have the chance again and your business will thrive by opening up to new people.

Unexpectedly, a business coach put her arm around me as we were walking through the hallway of the Women's Small Business Expo, held in Palm Springs, in April 2004, and said, *"If you are in business for yourself, you must increase your business exposure by becoming known as 'The Expert' in your field."*

Here is her recommendation on how to establish yourself as "The Expert" as well as earn the additional income you dream about:

• Write a book and an e-book version.
• Record informational CDs.
• Package attractively and sell.

By accepting help journeying through business development with others, I have come further in a given amount of time than I would have by myself.

Additionally, here is a list of the other pieces of the puzzle and new strategies I have learned as my business has developed:

> **Example:** *On occasion I will talk to groups of job-seekers on how to sell themselves in interviews, and to entrepreneurial students on how to build businesses.*
>
> • *Volunteer to give talks to groups about your area of expertise. My talks have been so well received, that I have been asked for return engagements and to set up workshops.*

> **Examples:** *Through one chamber of commerce, I was part of a Business Speakers' Series. To tie in with my brand, Smooth Sale, I'm working with another woman on developing sales training in conjunction with a cruise's event planner.*
>
> • *Host seminars by yourself or with a partner.*
> • *Announce the talks and seminars on websites and in local newspapers. The hosting organization will publicize the event. You may also write to editors of interested papers, magazines, and hosts of radio shows about your talk or seminar for free publicity.*

Example: I have been publishing a bimonthly Sales Tips e-zine for the past two years. Others have asked permission to reprint excerpts including a newly formed entrepreneurial organization in South Africa. A chamber of commerce has collected the newsletters in a notebook for their membership, and readers are asking me to write and send contributions to their periodicals.

• Write an informative website and publish an online newsletter on a regular basis.

Example: The more you get published (for free is always best), the more people will begin to recognize your name, and you will be viewed as "The Expert."

• Write articles for newspapers and magazines.

Example: Review radio stations locally and nationally that cater to an audience interested in your business. An online search may be the easiest way to find the information. Using Google, I entered "Local Radio Stations Bay Area" and one of the many entries that popped up was "Local Media/Radio Stations." This site listed radio stations, television stations, and newspapers for the San Francisco Bay Area.

• Obtain radio interviews.

> ***Example:*** *The certification allowed me to meet with large companies in regard to offering sales training. Without the certification, it would be far more difficult to get in the door. A big bonus has been networking with women already highly successful. By learning from them, my business has accelerated at "lightning speed" according to my associates.*
>
> • *Get certification as a minority- or woman-owned business.*

As you begin to gather attention and possibly fame, larger companies will find your services attractive and be more inclined to do business with you.

Key #2: Avoid Peaks and Valleys

Another lesson learned is that the peaks and valleys in sales are not fun. For those unfamiliar with the term, it means selling a large amount one month, followed by a dry month the next.

Gradually, better months come after a slow month and sales build, but then a dry spell will come again. Once you are in this cycle, it is continually repeated, hence the term, peaks and valleys.

Often this causes frustration and a feeling that you'll never be able to recapture the excitement and sales again. Earnings can be affected in a dramatic way as you get discouraged. Worst of all, thoughts of quitting come into play during this terrible cycle.

Years ago, I experienced this situation after I celebrated my big sale (outlined in the previous chapter). The following Monday, I worked hard in the morning, enjoyed a celebratory lunch with a couple of coworkers and then "took it easy" in the afternoon. On Tuesday, remembering the fun I had the day before, I repeated my laid-back agenda.

It became an easy habit to not work so hard. A week passed. In addition, the big sale required a great deal of follow-up both internally and with customers. And the paperwork was extremely time-consuming.

To ensure a smooth transition, I had to continually keep the new client apprised about delivery, arrange schedules for training, and then provide the training myself. There was no time left for prospecting. The combination of all these factors contributed to one long, bad month the following month.

It seemed to be more difficult than ever to find prospects. Almost no appointments were set. And certainly no business deals were closed the following month.

Adding insult to injury, not only was my commission nonexistent, but I missed out on the next quarterly bonus. At my company, it was necessary to hit minimum targets on a monthly basis. I made it a priority *never* to fall into this trap again.

> The moral of the story is to always prospect!

Work a normal routine every day. Always prospect for new business no matter what happens each day. Set the necessary time aside every day to phone prospective clients, follow up, and keep appointments.

Nice Girl Sales Tips

1. Look forward to each day.

2. Share the passion with your prospects and clients.
3. Let others help you.
4. Hold a helping hand out to those one step behind you.
5. Spread the joy with philanthropic activities.
6. Become known as "The Expert" through publicity, talks, and workshops.
7. Ask yourself, *"If I were the employer would I pay me?"*
8. Work each day to its fullest capacity—and prospect!
9. Schedule time off when you need it.
10. Compensate for anticipated time off.

6

Point Your Day toward Success

Make the most of each day with systems in place. These systems have several components:
- Routine
- Database contact management
- Manual backup
- Point system for activities
- Track the number of prospects versus the number of sales closed for your success rate percentage.

Develop a Daily Routine

In every industry, you need to develop a routine for maximum efficiency. Stick to a schedule as much as possible for phone calls, appointments, prospecting, and follow-up. Establishing this type of system allows you to begin each day efficiently. Planning the night before for the next day will give you a head start each morning.

There will be days where you will need to be flexible to accommodate change in the schedule. New appointments, deadlines, and unanticipated meetings all add to the mix.

A typical day will be making new and follow-up telephone calls in the morning from 8:00–9:30, followed by spending most of the day keeping appointments and prospecting for new clients. Late afternoon is a good time to follow up on requested information that is only available during business hours, as well as making follow-up telephone calls.

The evenings, unfortunately, are the best time to create proposals. Because proposals require considerable concentration and thought, you would waste all of your daylight selling hours if you were to compose them during the day.

The same is true for extensive mailings. Due to time consideration, mailings should also be completed in the evening or, you may consider employing a service to handle the mailing activities for you.

Providing you can concentrate on what you are writing, thank-you notes for appointments and for sales can be written while watching television.

Database Contact Management System

Between networking and contacting prospects, your desk will be piled high with business cards, notes, and tiny pieces of paper. You will have too many prospects and clients to remember when they are all to be contacted, what they said previously, where their new interest lies, or when the next appointment is to take place.

To avoid headaches and worry about losing valuable information, enter the appointments and interested parties into a database contact management system. If you are running a business, enter all contacts into the system.

Decide which type of database system works for you. Each system has integration features to make your office life easier. With further research, you will know which system is right for you.

Once you have your database system set up, enter every business person you have ever come into contact with into the system, and do it as soon as you receive the card. Someone once advised me to do that but I didn't listen.

Months later, I was playing "catch-up" with too many other tasks at hand. It became obvious that I was never going to catch up. Instead of having a handle on the situation, I found myself needing to either purchase a card reader or spend several hours typing in the information. By taking care of your contacts from the outset, you should be able to avoid this added expenditure or playing catch-up, which is so time-consuming.

It is also important to develop a monthly contact system. You can send email, notes, make phone calls, or just drop by in person to make sure that your clients are happy. Whichever method you choose, it is crucial to implement it for repeat business and referrals.

Use the calendar feature of your database contact management system to register any follow-up phone calls, appointments, and requested information. Add as many notes as possible so that you will have a running dialogue handy to refer to before contacting the prospect again.

Manual Backup

While technology makes our lives easier, it is important to note that it sometimes fails. Be sure to back up all your information on a weekly basis. In addition to the CD back-ups, keep a manual backup system, such as a day timer, for important phone calls and appointments.

A Point System for Your Activities

Your system should be tailored to your industry and to whether or not you sell full time. The system I recommend is based upon a full-time sales job in corporate America. For business development activities you will need to adapt the idea to your requirements.

Years ago, I was told that an average salesperson achieves fifty points per day. Never wanting to be average, I always strived to hit sixty to seventy points per day. No matter the combination of points, the system never let me down—it always worked.

It is this concentrated work effort that will help you to become a top producer and earn the rewards you are seeking.

The good news about working so hard is it leaves little time to be drawn into conversations bad-mouthing management or gossiping about others as most of my colleagues did. I worked hard all day. At night, I went home to my family. I looked forward to cooking dinner and eating it at the table where we each shared stories of our day's events. When I did talk to my colleagues it was either about business or the pride I took in my family. There was very little anyone could find to gossip about me. I came to be viewed as "the Nice Girl in the office."

Valuation of Point System
- An email is a 1/2 point.
- A telephone message is a 1/2 point.
- A telephone call is 1 point (lots of messages to the same person who is not responding do not count).
- A first appointment and a closing appointment are 10 points each.

- An intermediary appointment that furthers the sales process is 5 points.
- Mailers, and any other follow-up, are 1 point each.

Are you curious? Try tracking yourself for a week to see how much activity you are doing. Make adjustments where necessary. You will be very happy with the results.

If you are currently in business development mode, make certain you are focusing on those activities to complete them in an efficient and timely manner. Then as quickly as possible, return to the sales-related activities to grow your business.

Tracking Prospects Versus Closed Sales for Percentage

It is very important to understand your percentage of closes so that you will know if, and where, improvements need to be made. If you are in an office with others, ask your manager what the statistics are for the top sales executives. Then compare their numbers to yours.

Take the Nice Girl approach toward your manager by asking:

> *"I admire the work John Smith does and the results he gets. Would you please share with me everything he does in terms of numbers so that I can duplicate it to get the same results for you?"*

Once you put the request in terms of wanting to do this for your manager, you will be golden and the manager will do everything to help you.

Be honest with yourself and figure out whether you need to increase your activities or improve the ways in which they are implemented. If need be, read more books or listen to CDs on your subject. Ask for help or register for a class. Self-improvement is the best way to increase sales, along with perfecting your sales techniques.

Nice Girl Sales Tips

1. Operate with systems in place.
2. Devise a point system for your day.
3. Set a goal for the number of points you want to achieve.
4. Track all of your numbers.
5. Know what you need to do each day to improve.
6. Exceed what is needed each day in order to set records.

7
Manage Your Management

This is for those of you who are selling for a company over which you have no ownership. There are two sets of clients you need to sell to when working for a company. The obvious set is your prospects.

The second set you need to sell to is the management of your own company, beginning with the first level manager. There are several ways in which you can control how you are treated and what kind of perks you may receive. Most salespeople make the error of complaining about paperwork and impromptu meetings that take time away from the field. Some salesmen were known to use four letter words and rehash how crappy the company truly was. This only served to put everyone, especially management, on the defensive and in a bad mood. Everyone suffered from their bad behavior. Instead, use your inherent relationship-building skills and welcome these interruptions with a smile. Most often, these time wasters are due to top management being concerned about meeting numbers and financial requirements by the end of the month. Complying with management will instantly make you a favorite. In exchange for being so nice to work with, you will be thought of first when perks are to be handed out and spoken about in glowing terms to the higher-ups.

My worst experience as a saleswoman came in my third year. Yes, the third year of selling was even worse than the first year! I was now selling document management services to giant Silicon Valley companies.

My mistake: I did not know about selling to management.

My immediate sales manager, Dave, thought I was one of the greatest salespersons he had ever encountered. Unfortunately, I worked in concert with the sales manager, Dave, and a retail manager, Ann. I butted heads with Ann. Corporate and retail sales mix almost as well as oil and water. She pulled strings and the next thing I knew, it was written up in my personnel file that I was actually going to be fired for:

"Being a perfectionist and putting the client first!"

Working in this particular company was akin to working in the twilight zone. They were actually upset that I expected documents to be bound with all of the pages right side up, and that I insisted that missing pages were not acceptable. I was fighting my own company on behalf of my clients.

Friends in other industries told me, that if I had experience in the products they sold, they would hire me in an instant. But I didn't. It took years for me to recount this incident and be able to laugh about it.

Since management sticks together (it's a brotherhood), Dave, had nowhere to go but to side with Ann. I actually had to hire an attorney to save this insane job. I only wanted it so that I could interview well for the next one.

When I was ready to leave on my own terms, Dave told me that in sales, you always have to sell to management. What he meant was, I needed to learn to automatically do the following:

- Keep management abreast of all the activities in accounts of keen interest by volunteering the information.
- Provide quality input for improving my own sales and those of the team.
- Put blinders on in regard to negative corporate edicts.
- Process paperwork immediately.
- Keep a positive outlook for both myself and my teammates.

Never wanting to go through the aggravation of almost being fired again, I memorized those words of wisdom. This hard-learned lesson followed me into my fourth year of sales and beyond.

My attitude toward management made a 180-degree turn. As with my clients, I began to put myself into management's shoes and viewed the sales arena from their viewpoint. It worked beautifully.

I began to practice the relationship selling skills I used on clients on my new manager. His requests became incorporated into my agenda. The macho men were no longer in the spotlight. Instead, I became the one positively taking the spotlight throughout the company. Be aware that management can upset your planned day with unannounced paperwork that is very time-consuming. Unless you are on your way to an appointment, complete the paperwork immediately.

On a couple of occasions, at my fourth company, I thanked my manager for the form he unexpectedly handed to me. No one had ever thanked him before for extra paper-work, so imagine his delighted surprise!

After momentarily scanning the paperwork, I suggested that he wait a minute. I completed the paperwork while he stood there, and handed it right back to him. He relished the fact that I immediately acted upon his requests and used me as an example to the rest of our sales team. He also bragged about all of my endeavors to upper management, and how he single-handedly found and hired me.

As an extra perk for being the Nice Girl in the office, this particular manager would treat me and the other top producer in the office to lunch. It gave the three of us an opportunity to know one another better on a personal level away from the office. In most sales offices helping one another is a unique concept. My relationship selling to the manager and the revered male top producer resulted in developing a bond between us and re-enforcing the atmos-phere of camaraderie.

Should you use this suggestion, you will notice two pos-itive occurrences. The first is you won't have the guilt of not completing the paperwork and it will be out of your thoughts immediately. You can then continue with what you truly need to do to earn income.

Management will find more ways to sidetrack salespeo-ple by having them fill out unnecessary paperwork. At times they appear to be focused on minute details rather than on the big picture of devoting more time to selling hours and positively affecting the bottom line.

The second and best result (providing you are above quota and continue to respond with immediacy to paperwork) is that your manager will view you as a superstar. Your requests in the office will be granted cheerfully, and your name will be used at every opportunity as an example of an outstanding employee.

Upper management will become impressed with your capabilities. Completing paperwork immediately makes life in the office a very pleasant environment, particularly for you.

My manager couldn't praise me enough. He received his paperwork back, on average, within five minutes of giving it to me. I told him the meetings he held were interesting and that I always learned something new. I said it because it was actually true.

I helped others on the team without being asked. Plus, I was bringing previous clientele back, after they had been considered "lost." This manager thought I was the best all around representative he had ever encountered.

The following story proves the point about the importance of selling to your management:

A year into the job, I went to headquarters for a class. There was a woman sitting by herself so I went up to her to introduce myself with a smile and a handshake. Upon announcing my name, the woman looked astonished and, in disbelief said:

> *"You're Elinor Stutz? The Elinor Stutz? I thought that was a made-up name!"*
> *"What are you talking about?" was my response.*

I thought this woman had lost her marbles. She went on to say:

> *"All we ever hear at this office is how you turn your paperwork in immediately, actually enjoy and contribute to the meetings, can get into accounts that were lost, and sell to Fortune 100 accounts. Management uses your name at every opportunity."*

Needless to say, I was stunned. But as you can imagine, I was treated very well at that company. What a difference the original advice made! I truly was this company's *superstar*.

My manager was always in my court, backing me up and promoting me. I went on to win many awards and a great deal of recognition. It became such a wonderful job that it was hard to believe they actually paid me.

The extra piece of advice that I would add is, if there is a personality conflict between you and management, try to find a better fit elsewhere. Speaking from experience, it isn't worth the aggravation of hanging on to an unpleasant situation.

Nice Girl Sales Tips

1. Keep your manager happy.
2. Sell management on all of your activities. Always volunteer updated information on the status of your accounts.
3. Fill out time-consuming paperwork immediately.
4. Be a team player and help others.
5. Contribute to team meetings.

8
Manage Your Career

Although things were rapidly deteriorating at my third company, I was now quite confident in my ability. One day, I saw an advertisement for the position of "Major Accounts Manager."

Remember the first interview I described at the beginning of the book? The position advertised was for the very same company and branch office. I decided to go for an interview to play havoc with the man who bellowed at me to "get out," figuring the same person was still in charge.

To my delight, there was a very nice gentleman in the position of manager, and we hit it off. While the title of Major Accounts Manager felt above my capability, I decided I would grow into the position, and so when it was offered, I accepted.

As it turned out, the man I had expected to see had transferred to another office. (I still remembered the promise I muttered to myself when he had asked me in no uncertain terms to leave the premises.)

While my new manager was, overall, a very nice guy, he did a typical management maneuver during the interview. He altered the facts to get me in the door. I was told that by being a major accounts manager, I would inherit an account list of household name accounts. I would become very wealthy very soon! I was thinking "Wow, I've made it."

The story went that the previous salesperson had taken ill and could no longer work. (Note: He was probably ill from aggravation.) The new manager said he would have taken over, but he had just taken the manager spot, so it wouldn't be right to vacate his position so soon. The money would be galloping in and it would all be mine!

On Monday morning, I raced to work. I couldn't wait to start dialing for dollars and start that stream of income rolling in. As I began to dial, this is the message I heard over and over:

> *"I'm sorry, the number you have dialed has been disconnected and there is no new number. Please be sure to recheck the number in case you have dialed in error."*

I heard this message twelve times. I had been given a list of twenty-four "dynamite" accounts. Twelve accounts were out of business. Out of the second set of twelve, I heard one of two messages directly from the prospect's/client's mouth:

> *"We have never done business with your company before, and we never will."*
> *"We have done business with your company and trust me, we never will again!"*

I believe it was at this job when my hair started to turn gray.

I was terror-stricken not knowing what to do. I had just

quit a job where they had wanted to fire me; I had promised my husband I would help save enough money for our children to attend the college of their choice; and now I was stuck—in a new job where no one wanted to do business with my company.

That Monday night, I lay awake thinking about how to handle this. Do I start interviewing all over again and waste more time, or do I try to make sense out of what just happened?

That night I devised a plan for the next day.

I glanced back to the roots of my first sales job recalling the techniques that had made me successful as a novice. Building relationships as the Nice Girl jumped to the forefront. Then I recalled the advice, "Sometimes you need to fall on your sword." I tied all of my previous sales experiences together to move forward to execute my plan.

It seemed to me that if a company had previously conducted business with my company there had to have been a compelling reason to have done so, and there must have been a terrible slip up for which I needed to apologize.

On Tuesday morning, I began calling the six companies with whom my company had previously done business. My first statements were to assure them that I was new, was known for "putting the customer first," and that I wanted to hear firsthand from them what had happened.

Of the six companies, I only remember in detail what transpired at one large facility with a campus. This company worked with the federal government and with the California environment.

After hearing the prospect, Louise, rant and rave over the telephone, I apologized and assured her I did not work in the same manner as the previous salesperson. I asked for a meeting to talk more in-depth about what had transpired.

I showed up at Louise's office a few days later to find that she was away on an emergency. Although surprised she did not call to postpone the meeting, I called to make another appointment.

The second time I made an appointment with Louise, I was stood up again. A third meeting was set with Louise and I was stood up yet again.

Normally, having been stood up two times would have been enough for me, but this was a large company and provided very interesting services for California in terms of seismic activity. I wanted to learn more about the company and their services.

Since it was a government account, I patiently allowed more latitude for the meeting to take place. I really wanted to be able to say, *"This company is a client of mine."*

At the same time, while all of my newly inherited accounts were declining to meet with me, I was told there were doubts about my ability to sell. Management thought I should have had big sales by now.

Understand that management never wants to hear the real truth, such as you lied to me on the interview.

In their view, there is no excuse for not being able to sell. They have their goals to meet and regardless of what has happened previously, all of their salespeople must help achieve those goals.

At this point, I realized I needed to address the situation at the big account. So I called Louise back a fourth time and said:

> *"You must feel very guilty about standing me up three times."*

I heard an embarrassed giggle, and then went on:

> *"Once again, I apologize for all of the terrible misdeeds that took place in the past. All I'm asking for is five minutes of your time. If you do not like the way I look, talk, or dress, you have my permission to throw me out and I promise to never call you again."*

Success! We both kept the appointment and our conversation was quite friendly. There was a clock on the wall behind her desk. As I was in mid-sentence, I noticed five minutes had gone by, and said:

> *"Oh my goodness, five minutes have already passed. Would you like me to leave?"*

My directness and honesty took Louise by surprise. She admitted that she liked me and asked to continue the meeting. By the time the meeting was over, she asked me for a proposal. I could not have been more surprised.

That evening I worked on the proposal, passed it by my

manager (to his delight) and presented it to Louise the next day. For the next three months, Louise asked me at least bimonthly for a proposal.

However, while I was kindly thanked by Louise for each of my proposals, they were all turned down. The current vendor was, again, the best-known in our industry.

By the end of the three months, Louise asked:

> *"How come you are always able to provide me with a proposal within twenty-four hours of my asking for it, yet my current vendor takes from two weeks to a month to bring one in?"*

I replied:

> *"I am trying very hard to earn your business. I think it's time now for you to give me an opportunity. I'm not asking for you to acquire our largest system. Why don't you try a tiny desktop model to test the service I promise I will deliver? Then you will know if we are worthy of your business."*

My response impressed her. I was handed a request for a small desktop copier to be placed at their warehouse. The only drawback was that it was not in the best of neighborhoods.

I timidly walked down a dark alley while listening to barking dogs hoping they were behind strong fences. I was still determined to make this venture a success.

I met with the people at the warehouse, and talked with them for an hour. I got to know the employees well, and asked about the tasks they needed to perform on the job, and their preferences for a copier.

Louise was impressed by how much time I had taken and how much respect I had shown the employees. They had never been treated that well before, and called her to say they wanted to purchase only from me.

When the copier was delivered, I gave them the same courtesies I provided clients who purchased large systems. These warehouse employees again reported back to Louise that I was wonderful to work with and far more responsive than the current vendor.

A second request for equipment came my way from a second department on the main campus. I used the same process. I sat down to speak with everyone who would be using the system to find out exactly what would fit their situation best. I took every precaution to ensure a smooth transition to my equipment, ousting the previous vendor. I felt on top of the world!

By my ninth month on the job, I had the entire campus as my client except for the central copy center for very high volume duplication in which we could not compete. This account became one of my favorites over time.

If you find a method that works for you, keep doing it!

While the sales process was developing at that one company, I diligently began to again call the other five companies that had refused to conduct further business with the company I represented. One by one, I began to develop a relationship with each.

The other favorite account of those days was a well-known construction company that required copiers and fax machines at all their construction sites as well as at headquarters.

The same message was relayed to me that the representative before me had blown his chance for repeat business and it was unlikely my company would see any future business.

Repeating the process outlined above, I asked for an appointment. I listened to the buyer as he scolded me for all of the ill will produced before I came on board. I simply asked:

> *"What will it take to resolve the situation?"*

The buyer looked at me in complete surprise when he heard I actually wanted to take steps to resolve the past mishaps. Going a step further, I offered to make a notebook for him as a resource for the latest equipment on the market. Now he was truly amazed that I was planning to work to earn his business.

I then asked to meet not only the department heads at headquarters to learn how they used the equipment, but also to visit the construction sites to speak to the people there. The buyer now knew I was truly there to earn the business.

At this point, the same thing occurred as in the government account. I was granted a small machine as a test. If the copier performed well, and if I took good care of the client, and if my company delivered on promises, then I would have the opportunity to sell larger units on a frequent basis. From that point on, every month, I was called for requests for new equipment. Once again, I had replaced the best-known vendor.

In my opinion, it doesn't take much to get business when the competition puts in so very little effort.

The government and the construction accounts were my bread and butter. You had better believe I took excellent care of them. They received outstanding service and attractive pricing.

Applying the concept of vertical marketing—that is, concentrating on companies within the same industry—I began calling on other construction companies and visiting both their headquarter facilities and their trailer offices at the construction sites. It was a priority of mine to become familiar with their personnel and projects and to be viewed as a valued vendor. I also quickly became familiar with the industry's jargon, issues, and trends, which helped position me well for future sales. As announcements appeared in the newspaper about new building projects for which they were hired, I would call the purchasing manager to discuss upcoming equipment needs. He loved the fact I was on top of their business and assumed the role of partnering with him.

I also applied these same principles to government accounts. The service I delivered was impeccable. As a result, I was always welcomed.

Realizing the potential for continual repeat business, I kept the dollar amounts charged very competitive for these two types of accounts. The government accounts were on a GSA Schedule—special tiered pricing offered only to government offices. The pricing was set lower than traditional commercial accounts. Since the pricing was tiered, I was able to keep to the midrange level of what could be charged, as opposed to colleagues who always offered the lowest price available.

Charging a moderate price and delivering unparalleled service kept the clients very happy. My competitors could not even get in the door. I now understood the term "Order Taker,"—while I would be filling out paperwork at my desk, the phone would ring and I would hear:

> *"We're short a fax machine at the construction site— please deliver one ASAP."*

There was no mention of price or quibbling over minor details. My clients knew that a fair price would be charged and that the equipment would be received ASAP.

Every month, I exceeded my numbers and met my company's criteria for bonuses. The awards came in the form of recognition, gifts, cash, trips, and ultimately, President's Club. The sales methods I have described truly work well!

Knowing that I would be able to meet my quota every month from these two accounts, I was now able to add more profit into the new sales of new accounts each month.

I was now bringing Fortune 100 and 500 companies in the door, in addition to building a thriving repeat business base. My income, stature at my company, and confidence level were growing simultaneously.

Extra Pointers for Selling Items That "Plug In"

For those of you who sell products that "plug in," read the following section very carefully.

As accounts began to develop, I had to make absolutely positive that even when equipment failed, my clients would receive outstanding care. Particularly in the winter, when people tend to get the flu, and technicians may be on the sick list, I made certain my accounts would still receive the best of care.

I became friendly with the technicians and asked them what their challenges were at each account, how they were treated there, and how I might make their job easier.

Only the top salesperson in the office and myself cared about the technicians. Who do you think received the best care for their clients? Who do you think never lost an account and always made trips and bonuses?

> You must help those who help you.

Once the top salesperson realized I was serious about taking care of my clients and doing well for the company, he confided one tip that cinched my ability to provide outstanding care for my clients.

> *The secret to success was to pay a bonus, out of my own pocket, to the lead technician dedicated to the account.*

In those days, the technicians were barely paid minimum wage. There was somewhat of a resentment between them and the salespeople who appeared to be "raking it in."

So here is how my Bonus Program worked approximately ten years ago:

For every copier sold (no matter what size), I paid the lead technician for the account a $100 American Express check as a gift. For every fax machine there was a similar gift in the amount of $50.

The size of the units did not matter even though less profit would be made on smaller units. Over time, it all evened out. The main goal was to ensure that everyone was happy.

One added benefit to this bonus program was that an edict came down from management that the sales force had to teach the clients how to program the fax machines. I had no ability to do this, as I found the fax machines quite complicated. Additionally, I was selling a lot of them and the trainings would have consumed all my time.

The technicians were so grateful to be receiving the bonuses that they told me they would still teach the clients how to use the fax machines and not to worry about it.

The technicians and I became good friends and my clients loved all of us.

By taking care of everyone, everyone took care of me.

At this point, I was sending fruit baskets or bringing in candy after sales, taking clients out to lunch and writing many, many thank-you notes. President's Club, trips, and cash bonuses all became available to me.

Many times clients would hug me at the end of an appointment. My manager laughed when he looked through the office window one day and saw my client and I walking into a nearby shoe store after the client viewed the latest demo in our office. He said he had never before heard of a salesperson going shopping with a client!

What the manager and salesmen did not realize was we

were businesswomen on one level and girlfriends on another. This was a repeatable act with all of my clients. I had gotten to know Susan on a personal level. During appointments, I learned her concerns about her daughter. Later, I heard the triumph Susan felt when her daughter graduated college. Susan confided her own plans for retirement and which community she had picked out to live the rest of her life. Our conversations were highly confidential. Over time we delighted in seeing one another to trade secrets and share dreams. My relationship-building skills produced good friends in a highly competitive business environment throughout Silicon Valley.

I was loving my job, enjoying my new friends, and having a lot of fun. Out of the original ashes, a thriving territory had arisen. In corporate America, it was the best job I ever had.

Nice Girl Sales Tips

1. Keep trying.
2. Find alternative ways to accomplish your goals.
3. Once you find a method that works, keep doing it.
4. If your method is working, don't let anyone tell you it is wrong.
5. Building relationships and trust is the first step.
6. Apologize if you have to for the past behavior of others.
7. Give assurances about corrective actions.
8. Be aware of a prospect's time.
9. Get to know each person personally.
10. Find out each person's goals and needs, and meet them when possible.
11. Deliver the best service possible.

12. Make certain everyone from your team delivers the best possible service.
13. Establish bread-and-butter accounts to achieve your set goals.

> *Find and develop a handful of accounts that will buy from you repeatedly over time by being fair on the price and delivering exceptional service. The idea is to establish a steady clientele to meet your monthly quota or target, and to derive a steady income. Using the principle of volume buying, the pricing for these accounts will be a little lower than for the one time client.*

14. Add more profit into sales beyond your bread-and-butter accounts.

> *For those accounts where it appears:*
> - *You may only sell one time.*
> - *You are offering exactly what they need.*
> - *Your competitors do not have what the prospect needs.*

You now have the flexibility to charge more than you would if you anticipated repeat business and/or a good deal of competition. In order to accomplish this, you must sell value and service from the moment you set foot in their office.

Looking Good on All Levels

Once you have a client, and take excellent care of that client, you have the potential for repeat business and referrals—the easiest and the least expensive methods for acquiring business. You will want to do everything in your power to see to it that your clients are satisfied.

By value-add selling all the way through the sales cycle and by taking excellent care of your clients, you will build what Ken Blanchard termed "Raving Fans." In fact, *Raving Fans* by Ken Blanchard, (published in 1993 by William Morrow & Co.) is a book you should read, but only after you finish this one!

An accountant once shared that it costs approximately six times as much money to find a new client than it does to receive repeat business from a current client. By taking care of this one revenue stream, you will keep your management happy and reach your desired income.

To fully understand the concept, think about one particular service with which you enjoy doing business. For instance, when I need a "get well" gift, I immediately think of a particular company that provides food baskets.

Their service is immediate, both on the Internet and by dialing their 800 number. My address book is stored with them for added convenience. The food products are of outstanding quality and every basket has always arrived on time and in good shape. People always thank me and comment on the excellent quality of the food.

This company's value-add is at the end of processing the order:

> *"To show you our appreciation we would like to offer you a 20 percent reduction on anything in our store."*

The point is, I can always count on this company to take care of me and my friends, and to deliver quality service every step of the way. Every salesperson and businessperson needs to take their business to this level of excellence.

The acid test is to ask yourself, *"Would I pay out of my own pocket for the service my company and I deliver? Is it worth it?"*

If the answer is "no," then analyze where the improvement needs to take place and work on it until it is resolved. The only way you can successfully sell is if you fully believe you are providing a complete solution for the client.

For those who think they can bluff their way through an account, think again. Prospects are more knowledgeable than ever and they can sense if your own goals are the only thing on your mind. The passion and belief in what you do must come shining through.

How to Make Your Pipeline Bulge

While I now had six thriving accounts, it was necessary to have additional accounts in case of an unforeseen drop-off due to a change in personnel, poor economy, or the client company quitting business. Notice, I did not mention that the competition might take business away from me, and that is because I never allowed it to happen.

Still selling to my manager, I *requested* the opportunity to cold-call in my territory. I was his superstar. Since no one in their right mind would make such a request, my wish was immediately granted.

There were biotech companies, beautiful business parks, and a couple of Fortune 100 companies in my territory. I immediately began making the cold calls, with a focus on the larger companies.

Working those larger companies taught me a lot about strategic selling. In fact, if you are not familiar with the concept, make certain to read the book by the same name. Again, *after* you finish this book! This is also the market where I honed my relationship selling skills. In many cases I found myself doing a balancing act trying to advance my selling goals while being very careful to remain on good terms with everyone in the organization.

In many large companies, you will be told to call on the purchasing manager who makes the decisions about what to buy. In some cases this level has complete authority, but sometimes the "C" level (Chief Executive Officer, Chief Financial Officer) makes the final authorization. Additionally, other department heads may tilt the decision one way or another.

If you meet with the purchasing manager first, you are in jeopardy of walking on a tightrope. You do not want to offend the purchasing manager, yet you need to be able to cover all of your bases by ensuring that you meet with everyone responsible for and involved in the decision.

As part of strategic selling, organize a multipronged approach to the account. You are confident that a number of departments will make excellent use of what you have to offer. Your task is to find a "coach" in the account who will help you sell to other department heads.

My approach was to contact all the levels at the same time! This combined the strategic selling with the concept of top-down selling, to avoid any conflict.

Top-down selling strongly suggests beginning with the executive level of decision makers. The premise of top-down is that the sales cycle will speed up dramatically by starting with the "C" level officer—Chief Executive, Chief Financial, Chief Technology. The executive level has little time to waste so decisions are made quickly.

On the other hand, lower-level management may be fearful of making the wrong decision, so they take longer with each task to ensure their success. They will not want to pass you up the chain also for fear of losing their job. Therefore, beginning with the purchasing manager will most often produce a far longer sales cycle.

> I began with the highest levels and worked my way down.

If you do proceed to call at the top level, you will receive one of two answers. If the first answer is, *"Yes, please come on in, we were waiting for your call,"* be prepared to talk about their company's core efficiencies and everything else of importance to a CEO. You may wish to find a magazine, written for chief executives, which highlights their day-to-day issues. Anything you can speak to of interest to the CEO will make you a very likely candidate.

Being realistic, however, it is highly unlikely that the CEO was waiting for your phone call. More likely you will hear a second answer, *"That's not my job; you have the wrong person."*

You must immediately respond with a statement similar to this:

> *"Then please direct me to the person who will make the decision for this. If you do, I promise to never bother you again!"*

Next, call the recommended person and say:

> *"Hi, Joe Shugart suggested I call you. He said you would be the best person to help me."*

By using the top official's name and telling this person they were referred as "the best person to help you," the response usually is, *"How soon can you come in?"*

At times, it may not be entirely appropriate for you to speak with this level. I would call the executive anyway and say the following:

> *"Your company is a major player in its industry. The company I represent has the same status in its industry. I am convinced we can help your departments maximize their efficiencies and help them run more effectively. I'm Elinor Stutz with Apples2Oranges Company. If you will just share with me the name of the person in your company who makes these decisions, I promise not to bother you any more!"*

Humor always worked for me.

The CEO would laugh, sigh, and then, unsure whether or not I was a stockholder, would give me the name of the person in charge.

The beauty of using this method was, by the time I contacted the purchasing manager, who might tell me, *"I make all the decisions, so don't bother anyone else,"* I would respond with:

> *"I was so looking forward to working with your company, I took it upon myself to already contact your CE. He kindly shared the name of your IT Director with whom I have an appointment on Tuesday. I hope you don't mind as I would very much like to meet with you also to learn your priorities for working with vendors."*

This message is informative as well as honest. The purchasing manager is now fully aware of those I have contacted, and the chain of command in which the calls were conducted.

However, the above statement also recognized the purchasing manager as a VIP and brought him or her to the same level as the others, and confirmed that his or her priorities are important and will be adhered to. The forgiveness for not having contacted the purchasing manager first should be forthcoming.

While a couple of purchasing managers were mildly annoyed that they hadn't been contacted first, it was easier to live with their annoyance than to have been stalemated in the accounts. This approach neither prevented me from proceeding nor from obtaining the sale.

It is very important in medium- to large-sized companies to have everyone on the same page and understand what it is you have to offer. When you find your first contact who appears to be friendly and helpful, ask if he or she can introduce you to everyone else involved in the decision-making process.

Systematically meet with all of the individuals who are mentioned. Make certain to keep the first contact in the loop about what transpires during the meetings. Send recaps of the highlights and a thank you for each introduction.

By the time a proposal is ready to be presented, you will want to have everyone involved in the decision-making process present at the final meeting.

The next important step is to hold the meeting, find out the next steps that need to be taken to advance the sale, and report back to the top official who originally spoke to you.

Write a brief note thanking the top official, letting him or her know you took their recommendation and conducted a successful meeting. Note the professionalism of the meeting and the final outcome. Take it one step further by recapping two highlights of the meeting. This will let the top official know you are easy to work with, thoughtful, and a potential new vendor.

You might also state that it will be a pleasure to work with their company. Send a duplicate copy to each person with whom you met.

Any communication you have with the CEO from this point onward, let your contact know about it in a friendly manner to prevent them from ever thinking you have gone behind their back. But keep the executive communication at a minimum.

The next best time for communication may be an invitation for the CEO to attend your final presentation. But first you will have to suggest to your contact that you would like to extend the invitation to the CEO.

If you were to begin the sale initially with a purchasing manager, you might never get to the top to find out what the burning issues are and what the final determination will be based upon. It would be bad form to go over the purchasing manager's head if you began the cycle at that level. Understand that even though the chief executives make the final approval, they receive input from the purchasing manager. If you inadvertently insult a purchasing manager, you will be history. This is one area where utilizing relationship building by being nice and respectful of everyone is essential.

I used every strategy I knew to entertain a Fortune 100 account famous for its credit cards. I accomplished everything described above. The purchasing manager required many, many hoops to be jumped through to the point of almost being insulting. Had it not been such a well-known account, I might have given up. But I wanted, once again, to be able to say, *"I sold to them."*

Realizing I was getting nowhere fast over a year's time, I had not only called on higher-level executives but also on lower-level executives. Most of the local department managers and executives knew who I was. Luckily, the executive level was housed at another campus and so I was able to call on them without offending the purchasing manager.

My management was impressed by how far I had gotten within the account. I had even brought specialists in to talk to the higher-level officers. But the assistant purchasing manager was still keeping me out. This account became a thorn in my side, since to that date it was the only company that would not let me in.

Timing is everything. During this process of trying every method I could think of to get into the account, my company announced that it was being purchased by a major company. Additionally, the new company would be buying many of our smaller competitors. What this meant to me was the sales reps selling complimentary and competitive equipment to ours were moving into our offices. On a down note, my original team found we had to lock our desk drawers and take the important files home every night, otherwise they would be stolen by the new folk who were envious of our earnings.

On a positive note, one of the newcomers was a woman who represented another line of fax machines. Julie was routinely selling into the account where I was having so much difficulty. Her contacts were different than mine. I had to step back to weigh my desire to sell into the account with her help against the anger and suspicion building in the office.

Rather than avoid Julie and all the other newcomers as my teammates did, I used my relationship-building skills to befriend her. I saw grand opportunity and laid out my plan for her. Once again I was working for a win-win solution as it is the proven way to motivate another.

I represented a fairly expensive line of printers and duplicators. My company was known for paying excellent commissions on this particular line. Julie was offered a generous 50-50 split on commission assuming I made the sale. All Julie would need to do to receive the split would be to introduce me to the people in the company to whom she was already selling. Julie recognized a golden opportunity too. Her reward would be almost infinitely higher than any commission she had ever earned. We became fast friends through the process.

There are always exceptions to the rule of selling at the top level of chief officer. While it is almost always important to start at top levels and work your way down as well as strategically sell, on rare occasions it is the least likely person on the totem pole whose vote counts more. This is another reason to be mindful of showing respect and kindness to everyone.

Julie introduced me to the people in the company duplication center. One day the copy center manager, who was housed in the basement, let me know their new requirements for a color system.

My eyes bulged out of my head. This dear man was describing the latest, biggest, fastest machine that just came out on the market. We were the only vendor able to offer what he had just described!

The news got even better. While the best-known vendor was this client's preferred vendor, their system could not perform the requirements the client set, while ours could. The other vendor implied they might be able to meet the requirements but we knew their specifications in-depth and explained them in detail to our potential client.

You must always find your competitor's Achilles' heel.

When I say "we," I mean that realizing the enormity and importance of this sale, I brought in the manufacturer's representative to help me out on the intricate specifics. He added tremendous credibility and value throughout the process of the sale.

And even better, my company organized an upscale equipment show. It was an opportunity to show potential clients that our company was doing well by hosting demonstrations at a prestigious local hotel. We were able to offer hospitality and delicious delicacies while prospects tested our equipment and spoke to the executives. The event brought more prospects in than an ordinary open house hosted at the office would have.

Hearing the news that I had this credit card company coming to the show, *all* of management showed for the event. They looked like proud peacocks when I walked in with my prospect. The prospect later confessed he had never received such fine treatment.

I only made one error in judgment within my own company. I gossiped. One of the trainers liked me and we became friendly. Over the course of time, I told her about my "crock of sh..." interview. She howled.

When I walked into the middle of the hotel room, my client was escorted by the manufacturer's representative to the color unit in which he was interested. Meanwhile, the C.O.S. (crock-of-sh..) manager pulled me over to a huddle with him, two of the vice-presidents and my confidant, the trainer. He said:

> *"Elinor, how could you have told the trainer that I yelled at you on an interview and said that your résumé was a crock of sh..? That's simply not true."*

I saw the elite group staring at me and awaiting my answer. Glancing back at the offender, I responded:

> *"Have any of you, in the past year, ever heard me speak like that? That type of language is not in my vocabulary and so it certainly isn't something I could even make up!"*

Everyone nodded and agreed. The trainer looked at him and said she could hear him saying those words. His face turned a dark crimson red.

> Your vocabulary is unique to you and will identify you, as it did him.

This turn of events made my day! And better yet, my prospect loved the equipment being showcased. Once again, I made certain my prospect was well taken care of, by being attentive to his questions and concerns. I introduced him to each of the executives of my company and saw to it that he was well-fed. This fellow was ecstatic.

The assistant purchasing manager at the credit card company always gave me a bad time. She absolutely disliked me, but happened to be out on vacation at the time. The temporary position was filled by a very sweet person who wrote me a note stating how appreciative they were of the fine care I showed their employee. Timing is everything!

Julie and I were able to place a very large color duplicator in the copy center basement. The service and supplies contract added considerably to the total bill.

Our best known competitor was once again outsold, and in a very prestigious account. It was one sale where I was extremely happy to split the commission.

Julie and I both came out very well by combining forces. I didn't have the right contact and she didn't have the equipment to sell. In this case, we had the perfect partnership.

Nice Girl Sales Strategy Recap

• Work to keep your management happy.
  - Keep them abreast of activity in your accounts.
  - Volunteer to do extra work.
  - Proactively turn in paperwork.
  - Introduce decision makers to your management.
• Become adept with strategic and top-down selling.

Nice Girl Sales Tips

1. Read *Strategic Selling* by Stephen Heiman.
2. Implement strategic selling and top-down selling skills.
3. Call many people at an account to find the one who will let you in.
4. Cater to your prospects and clients as appropriate.
5. Don't gossip.
6. Look for alliances within your own organization.
7. Value-add sell throughout the sales cycle.
8. Value-add sell after the sale.
9. Set your goal to obtain repeat business and referrals.
10. Extend the happiness to your office.

9
Selling Tinkerbell

Do you remember, as a child, seeing the movie, *Peter Pan*? The most important part of the movie, as far as sales is concerned, was when you were told:

> *"Clap your hands real hard or Tinkerbell will die!"*

Did you clap your hands? You were then told:

> *"Please, truly believe; clap your hands even harder. I think Tinkerbell is coming back alive!"*

As corny as this may sound, this is how you have to view the sales process. In particular you have to have the same unshakable faith in yourself and in the product or service you are selling.

You know that what you have is the right solution, but you must figure out a way to get the point across to your prospect.

Important notes:

- If you do not believe in yourself you will not be able to sell.

- You must believe in what you are selling.
- You must act with integrity, as a Nice Girl would—
otherwise you have nothing to sell.

Mid-career in sales, I had an entire city, in the heart of Silicon Valley, as a client. The economy was very good at the time. I had made friends with each of the department managers and the purchasing manager. I was able to demonstrate the value of upgrading from stand-alone copiers to networked printers. Gradually, each department upgraded as the leases for the older equipment came due. How was I able to establish trust with each department head?

Using the Nice Girl philosophy, my first visit to each department was merely to introduce myself to each of the decision makers. *"I want you to be able to put a face with a name,"* I said, when calling each person for the first appointment. Most importantly, upon arriving at their office, I offered to first resolve all outstanding issues before beginning a new sales cycle. They looked at me in complete amazement and asked me to return for a full appointment.

Why was this the case? This is the exact opposite methodology implemented by most other salespeople. They immediately begin trying to sell new equipment without ever getting to know the person behind the title first, or how their own company has been performing on the behalf of the client up until that point in time. Most other salespeople do not truly care about their clients. This is the exact opposite of the Nice Girl philosophy. Others are only concerned about the potential commission dollars and that message smacks of lack of integrity in the mind of the prospect. Their methodology most often turns out to be a huge blunder.

On the second appointment, in each department, I asked many questions. It was imperative to know what they did, what their goals were, if they interacted with other departments, and what types of documents they produced. Again, I asked about difficulties with their current equipment and if any issues needed to be resolved.

The Nice Girl approach is to dig for problems that need to be resolved whereas others avoid the problems at all cost, including the sale. For them, problems do not exist. By acknowledging that my company wasn't perfect but we were there to help fix anything that might have gone wrong, I became a heroine. My credibility and integrity were sky high. Not only did I enjoy the status, but I also became acutely aware that any talk of competitors completely subsided. The Nice Girl approach made this city account mine.

The results were that all of the department heads liked me for taking a keen interest and respected me for wanting to resolve issues before I attempted to sell anything new. I was then asked to inform them about the new printers and bring in proposals. Once again, the Nice Girl methodology produces the opposite result for what normally occurs. Rather than me insisting a prospect consider my proposal, I was always asked by my prospects to "please" bring in a proposal. By being a Nice Girl and having carefully developed the relationships, I knew ahead of time my prospects would shortly turn into clients. My management loved that I could accurately predict the sales that would close by the end of the month; that the margins were high; and my stress level was greatly reduced compared to that of other salespeople. Gradually every department changed equipment except for one.

The lone holdout was a very nice woman, Sally, who was close to retirement age. Sally only wanted to quietly do "the usual" until her last day of employment. I visited with her on a monthly basis, even though she had no interest in upgrading. However, I just knew I could save Sally and the rest of her staff so much time, which she often complained they did not have.

If only I could think of a way to motivate Sally to try to understand what printers were all about. Finally, I had a Nice Girl idea. I said to her:

> *"One of your offices that upgraded is only two blocks away. May I pick you up at noontime, one day next week, have a sandwich waiting for you, and drive you to that location? I promise not to say a word. I want you to play with the equipment and talk to the people who use it. If you are still not interested after that, I will not bother you about it any longer."*

Sally could not believe I would make such a generous offer to her. She took me up on it. I brought Sally over to the other office. Being a Nice Girl, I also kept my promise by not saying anything as she spent time playing with the equipment. By the time the half hour was over, her response was:

> *"I was such a fool. This would save us a lot of time and I will be able to do the other things that pile up on my desk. Thank you!"*

As we pulled up to Sally's office, she asked me to prepare the paperwork for not only a networked printer but also a desktop color printer. When I returned to my office and told my manager about the day's occurrence, he responded:

> *"I can't believe it. I had that account before you, and Sally was so bullheaded, I couldn't get to first base. I gave up!"*

Make a mental note—Nice Girls do not give up, instead, they find a better way!

One day the purchasing manager for the city, who approved all of the purchases for each department, confided in me:

> *"Every day, I get at least three calls from your competitors. They assure me I am spending too much on networked equipment and say they could save me a lot of money. But deep down, I know I would be a fool to let anyone else in because you take such good care of us."*

The purchasing manager confirmed the Nice Girl philosophy—take excellent care of your clients, show you care, and you too will be able to sell at higher margins. This philosophy encompasses the ideal sale, a win-win solution where everyone is happy.

> Build rapport and trust first.
>
> Customer service deeply affects your bottom line.

Nice Girl Sales Tips

1. At any point in the cycle, volunteer to resolve issues where necessary before introducing new services. This is the most important step, as it immediately builds credibility. This technique will most certainly put your competition on the defense, or may eliminate them entirely.

2. Ask questions to determine where their interests lie.

3. Bring value to the table with knowledge, patience, and a desire to solve problems. This point is very important. Your first appointment with a prospect is to uncover problems and their consequences so the prospect might take action by acquiring your service. At any point, a current client may become unhappy. By taking immediate action to solve problems, you will earn a lifetime client. Assuming you solve the issue quickly and fairly, the client will tell their associates, and you will reap repeat business, referrals, and testimonials.

4. Get the client to tell you what they want.

5. Deliver what the client wants.

6. Let the client know they can always count on you to follow through.

> Resolving issues is a major factor for your success.

Nice Girl Perseverance

A client, who was in charge of a copy duplication service for a very large legal firm in San Francisco, was furious with the performance of the equipment on his premises. Jim did not want me to come in to introduce myself as the new representative from my company. In fact, Jim wanted nothing further to do with my company. I assured Jim that I would not speak about newer, better, or faster equipment until all of the earlier problems were solved, and I kept my word.

Upon our first meeting, I said:

> *"I'm here to solve previous problems."*

He angrily pointed to the first piece of equipment my company had sold him and said:

> *"This never worked properly from day one, and I was ignored."*

I smiled, then responded:

> *"That's wonderful!"*

Jim looked at me as if I were crazy—until I exclaimed:

> *"This is not our equipment—it's our competitor's!"*

Jim's finger-pointing continued around the room to all the faulty equipment and each time, I smiled knowingly.

All of the problems he pointed out were that of our competitor's. Had I not taken the time to find out the truth, I would have lost out on new business. Not only was I now given the green light to proceed with beginning a new sales cycle and to write a proposal for new equipment, but my company was now also regarded in a highly favorable light.

Conclusion

Treat objections from your prospects with keen interest. Resolving issues appropriately will earn you lifetime clients and, very possibly, referrals. Few businesses today act promptly or with integrity. If you do, you will be very highly regarded and well on your way to successful smooth selling!

10
Creative Entry into Accounts

Definition of a Cold Call: Contacting a person whom you do not know, whether in person or by telephone, for the purpose of introducing yourself and asking for an appointment.

Definition of a Warm Call: Contacting a person you do know or contacting a referral by a third party and asking for an appointment.

Midway Point Between Cold and Warm Calls: Obviously it is far easier to proceed with a warm call, so you will want all the know-how on turning your cold calls into warm calls. At the very least, you want to start at the midway point. You will find suggestions on how to begin new phone calls at the midway point in this chapter.

In the Field

This is a more old-fashioned way of cold-calling. You seek out business parks or districts that appear to be thriving. Look for the obvious: cars in the parking lot and lights on in offices.

Due to security issues today, fewer buildings are accessible for cold-calling, particularly in the bigger cities. Do not try to cold-call in a building where your ID is requested.

The following ideas are for a more relaxed area where people walk about freely.

As you canvass, look for smokers or delivery people outside. They will usually answer questions you ask about the company and may even tell you who the decision makers are.

When I first began to sell, I was horrified to think I would walk unannounced into an office and disrupt the employees' work to ask questions. Worse yet, all of the offices posted signs that said "No soliciting."

My first day out, I was only able to find a couple of offices without the "No soliciting" sign. Upon my return to the office, I showed the manager only two business cards. My explanation of the "No soliciting" sign sent him into fits of laughter. Of course, all the men joined in as well to point out a Nice Girl couldn't possibly sell. I had to accept the fact you need to be blind to the "No soliciting" signs. Being the Nice Girl, not wanting to offend anyone, that was a very difficult behavior change for me and I found it scary.

Finally, a turn came when a trainer suggested we think of cold-calling as participating in a game show, striving to find *"What's behind the secret door?"* As soon as I switched the thinking around in my mind to view cold-calling as a game, I looked forward to each day.

Attitude is everything!

Cold-calling actually became fun and was a way to get out of the office. I played detective, looking for clues behind each office door to get to goal. Once again, setting your mindset to a positive outlook truly works.

By this time, I had discovered that in tall buildings it is best to start on the top floor, away from the property management office (they hate salespeople) and the guard. Once in an office, I quickly got the information I was seeking in a professional, low-key manner and left. Only once in the ten years that I cold-called was I asked to not return or they would call the police.

Side Note

One sales manager, whose knowledge I usually admired, disagreed with my method for cold-calling. He believed that I should leave more than a card with the receptionist. Flyers and brochures, in his mind, were the appropriate items to leave behind for the receptionist to pass along to the decision makers.

My Nice Girl thought on the subject is, when cold-calling, you are truly disrupting the people in the office. They aren't going to want to do your job of passing your information along.

Also, keep in mind, you are not the only person dropping in and making this type of request. It gets old for the receptionist and may be even awkward for him or her to present your card to the right person. Even worse, you become like everyone else who is requesting the same intrusive service. The best strategy is to differentiate yourself from everyone else at the very beginning of the selling process.

You want to differentiate yourself.

The Nice Girl philosophy is to treat everyone with equal respect as each individual is capable of making or breaking your advancement within a company.

By not asking for favors, but being polite and to the point, you will be more likely to get ahead. I found very good success in getting the receptionist to help in subsequent calls by treating him or her with respect. The easiest and most courteous way to receive the help of an administrative person is to politely introduce yourself and ask their name. From that point on call them by their proper name. Asking a person's name is one tiny, extra step that will bring a smile to their face. From that moment on, help for you is on the way. Most salesmen disregard this step unless it's a "cute" receptionist. I always graciously acknowledged every ounce of help they gave such as simply supplying the name of the right person for me to contact. The receptionists always put me through to their recommended point of contact whereas competitors gave up in frustration of not being able to get through.

Read the local papers of your territory and determine which companies are thriving and where business is done. For instance, just this morning, I read that one company doubled their earnings for the quarter due to advertising revenue. This should be an instant incentive for salespeople to contact the company as it is rapidly growing and will require new services.

Here is another example of knowing your territory. In Menlo Park, California, venture capitalists are known to have their offices located on one particular street, Sand Hill Road. If venture capitalists are your target market, then you would know to visit every office on that street.

Your entry into each office should entail the following Nice Girl process:

- Be swift with the least amount of disruption as possible.
- Ask, *"I was wondering if you can help me."* It's rare where a receptionist will say, *"No."*
- Get the appropriate contact information at as high a level as possible.
- Make certain you ask and write down the name of the receptionist. This person may be the spouse of the CEO. At least 80 percent of businesspeople overlook this fact. If your competition treats the receptionist as a low-level employee without importance, your competition will face a difficult time getting an appointment.
- Thank the receptionist by name for his or her help. Let the receptionist know you will follow-up immediately and then promptly leave. After the visit, when you do call the office of the person referred to you, make certain to greet the receptionist by name. Remind them you were just in the office, you are following up on their advice to reach the person they recommended, and thank them once again for their help.

The receptionist is the "gatekeeper," but will put you through because you are now liked and known as the Nice Girl.

True Story
Upon calling one such receptionist, I identified myself and said I was following up on her recommendation to contact

Louise Allen. The receptionist actually ran down the hallway to get Louise to return to her office to take my call. This was all her idea, not mine. I was very appreciative. Louise liked the fact her receptionist and I had such good rapport. She very willingly set an appointment with me.

On the Telephone

Your well-being comes through the telephone. If you are feeling down, unsure, or insecure, do not call. Wait until your spirits are up.

If you are unsure of what to say and how to say it, because you are new at this, there is another way to sound positive and energetic. Standing up while you are on the phone helps to improve the sound of vitality in your voice, and a smile on your face will enhance your friendliness over the phone. Some salespeople go as far as looking into a mirror to double-check they are smiling while talking to prospects on the phone.

Immediately after exercising is one of the best times to make difficult calls. The adrenaline is still pumping and will make you sound excited about what you have to offer. Another good time to call is right after you have succeeded with a task, received good news, or had a fun phone call with a friend or client.

The energy you send through the wires will be well-received and your chances for an appointment will jump dramatically!

If you are beginning the sales cycle on the telephone to a receptionist, announce who you are, why you are calling, and ask the receptionist's name. Then ask:

> *"Would you please tell me who makes the final decision for...?"*

and:

> *"May I be connected to him or her now?"*

Now that you have the name of the person to call, what do you say?

- Have you done your homework?
- Do you know something about their company, their competitors, or their industry?
- Have you contemplated issues they may be facing, and thought out how they could possibly take advantage of what you are selling?

Remember to listen carefully as the other party picks up the telephone and announces his/her name so that you may repeat it back correctly. For example, you are told to call Jennifer Brown. Yet, you hear:

> *"This is Jenny."*

You should immediately respond:

> *"Hi Jenny." or "Hello Jenny."*

Understand, in today's business climate, people lucky enough to still have jobs are literally doing the work of two or three people. They are not likely to want to talk to you.

In fact, the moment you announce who you are, they are most likely in the process of slamming the receiver down to hang up the phone.

This is the point where your small company can get the appointment even though their current vendor is a larger company. This is the exact moment where you need to get through by being different.

Instead of announcing your name and company, pose a question.

A possible question for many industries may be:

"Are you tired of having service issues transferred to foreign countries?"

Followed by:

"Would you prefer local service, or U.S. service?"

or

"Are you on a first name basis with your vendor?"

Followed by:
• (If the answer is "Yes")

"Is that because you are incurring so many problems?"

• (If the answer is "No")

> *"Would you prefer more attention from your vendor?"*

What happens is the other person's brain will begin processing an answer to your question while you are announcing your name and your company's name. The question will spark a short conversation. The answer comes forth honestly, because you caught the prospect with their guard down.

Now, as you announce yourself, you are able to follow up with:

> *"We can provide personalized service. I would be happy to come in to discuss how we can relieve your frustrations with service. How about next Tuesday or Thursday—which day do you prefer?"*

On your return visit to the office, greet the receptionist by name and thank her or him for helping you to obtain the appointment.

Your listening skills need to be very sharp for successful use of the telephone. This is where the Nice Girl philosophy comes in to play again to further the selling cycle. You need to hear whether the phone is picked up in a harried manner. If the party sounds agitated, acknowledge how busy they must be and ask:

> *"Is this a good time for you?"*

If the answer is:

> "No, this is not a good time,"

Then ask:

> "When might be a better time to call you back?"

Write down the time and date they give you, and note it in your records along with the original date and time of your first call. The next time you call, remind them that on the fourth of March they asked you to call on this date at this particular time. They are now obliged to talk to you.

Use Telephone Messages to Your Advantage

When leaving a message, it is very important to leave your phone number near the beginning of the message and once again at the end of the message. There are three reasons for this method.

1. People are busy and may not want to listen to the full message. By leaving your number early, they will have it for easy access.

2. Sometimes numbers are muffled. By leaving the number twice, it is highly unlikely the same number will be blurred.

3. By leaving the number at the end, the recipient will not have to replay the message to get the entire number.

NOTE: In the anxiety of the moment, if you forget to leave your number at the beginning of the message, the next best thing is to leave your message twice in a row in the middle or at the end in the following manner.

> "...I may be reached at (415) 615-6887. Again, the number is (415) 615-6887."

Leaving a phone message is a great tool if you do not wish to get into a lengthy conversation but need to confirm a request of your prospect or client. Generally speaking, Monday mornings and Friday afternoons, are the best times of the week to leave a message.

Employees no longer have the luxury of time to return telephone calls. Assume that unless you catch the person at their desk, you will need to keep telephoning or combine the telephone messaging with other methods.

Add Email for Extra Emphasis and Response

If the point of the message is a date that I am trying to arrange, in my message I say:

> *"I will email a duplicate message as it might be easier for you to press the 'reply' button rather than return the call."*

I immediately go to the computer and type the identical message spoken over the telephone. At the top of the message, I reference the telephone call. I also let the prospect know to choose a date and time for me to confirm. Keep the message short!

You will find the Nice Girl method of considering the prospect's situation before your own produces excellent results.

Clients appreciate the thoughtfulness of sending a duplicate email for ease of use.

I have *always* received a response using this strategy.

Recently, several prospects asked me to call them to set meeting times. I proceeded to call once, twice, and even three times but did not receive a response.

After the third message, I sent a short message via email. Almost immediately, the responses came back with a suggested date for meeting. Additionally, these prospects *thanked* me for my friendly persistence!

However, we have all embarrassed ourselves with email mistakes. For this reason, I strongly suggest you use caution when emailing. My suggestion is to type your email and use spell check, but do not send the message. Get up from your desk for a few minutes to take a short break.

When you return to your desk read the email out loud. This technique will let you know if you left out a word and if the sentences are well-constructed. Make certain your attachments are truly attached, and that you salutation has the correct name of the person intended.

Reviewing the email before sending it will save you from embarrassment.

Secrets Revealed for Finding Email Addresses

For a very short while, I endured inside sales. Compared to outside sales, sitting in a cubicle day after day was very boring and tedious.

Over time, email addresses became guarded secrets. Receptionists on the telephone sounded as if I were requesting social security numbers. How was I to get in touch with the appropriate person if they would not answer the telephone and I could not get their email address?

It is essential to be creative and seek alternate methods to get the information you need at each stage of the sales cycle. The first and most obvious place to find an email address is on the website of a larger company. Look for the corporate officer page. Very often the email address is listed beside a picture of each officer. Routinely, the company will follow that protocol for the email of all employees. So, if an officer's email address reads john.doe@mycompany.com, your contact's email address will most likely read betty.johnson@mycompany.com.

I began to play a game of "Guess their email address" for those companies that did not list the corporate officers and their email addresses. It occurred to me that in general, men refer to each other by their last name while women refer to each other by their first name. Therefore, the emphasis on their own email might reflect the same.

In my game research, I found that women will most often adopt an email address reflecting their own first name followed by @ the company, such as betty@mycompany.com. Next, they will add a last initial to read bettyr@mycompany.com. Occasionally, women will use both their first and last names either run together or separated by a period or underscore.

Men, on the other hand, will begin with their last name at the company (doe@mycompany.com) and secondly use their first name initial followed by their last name (jdoe@mycompany.com). After these first two choices, then their email will be similar to the women's email addresses by combining their first and last names separated by a period or an underscore to read as john.doe@mycompany.com or john_doe@mycompany.com.

The beauty of all this is that, although there are five possible combinations you might try to get through, it only takes a couple of minutes to find the right one. Incorrect addresses usually bounce back immediately, and so you will know fairly quickly if one actually gets through. Make certain to only try one address at a time just in case more than one gets through. A Nice Girl does not want to be mistakenly identified as a spammer!

If you have an important message to get across, it is certainly worth the effort to test the variations of email addresses.

Holiday Calls in the Field

Holiday time is the best time to visit clients and potential clients in the field. This is the ultimate time for putting your Nice Girl relationship selling skills to work. Almost everyone is in a jovial mood and, if treated correctly, they will provide all the information you wish to know.

A number of years ago, I had successfully sold into an aerospace account in Palo Alto with the nicest people as clients. Over time, we became friends and got to know each other well. By putting their interests first, I was able to develop a lot of repeat business.

Two years later, I changed both employers and territories. To my delight, another one of the company facilities was now in my new territory in Sunnyvale. I couldn't wait to visit this new site and share my knowledge of their company.

To my dismay, there was one major difference between the two facilities. The Sunnyvale plant was rigidly secured by a guard who could have doubled for a pit bull. He had tattoos up and down his arms, guns at his hips, and a mean snarl. This man actually frightened me.

Management knew this plant was in my territory. There was no way I could tell them I was afraid of the guard for fear he might bite! This was a huge dilemma for me.

The days passed and Halloween came. I purchased a large bag of miniature candy bars from Costco. Every year, I methodically gave a candy bar to receptionists at each office that I visited, to wish them a very happy holiday season and new year. (Remember, I was called "The Bulldozer"!)

This Halloween day, I approached the plant, pulled into the driveway and parked. For ten minutes, I tried to convince myself that it was safe to get out of the car and greet the guard.

Reluctantly, I opened the car door, grabbed a candy bar, and, in slow motion, approached the door of the plant. Still afraid, instead of walking up to the guard's desk, I stood in the doorway and threw the candy bar at him as if he were a caged animal. At the same time, I shouted, *"Happy Halloween!"*

At that very moment, the most unusual reaction occurred. This guard, who had frightened me beyond comprehension, had tears streaming down his face. He was actually crying!

Through sobs, the guard managed to say:

> *"No one ever gave me anything before. Thank you so much!"*

Finally composed, he continued:

> *"I bet you want the names of the decision makers in this plant. Here, take my book into the ladies' room. But don't let anyone see you. Take your time and write down all the names you want."*

Hallelujah! I gladly took the guard's book to the ladies room, locked the door, and wrote down all the names I could find. After returning the book, I went to the car to retrieve a few more candy bars, gave them to the guard, thanked him again, and wished him the best holiday yet.

Any doubts about the sale? The contacts on the receiving end of the call were so amazed I was able to get through to them; they figured I must be good! I was invited in with warm hospitality.

The Nice Girl philosophy says to remember even though company employees have titles, decision making rests in the hands of all employees. Treat everyone with equal respect.

Unique Mailings
The last method for gaining entry into new accounts is to send attention-getting mailings. The cost of postage adds

up for large mailings, so I suggest this strategy only for salespeople who will be able to get their company to pay for postage.

On the other hand, if you are still inclined to send mailings to your prospects and clients, as long as you can attract interest, it is certainly worthwhile doing.

To make certain your designated contact opens the mailing, the envelope must look personal in nature, not like throwaway literature. There are several ways to do this.

• Instead of manila envelopes, use white envelopes.
• Purchase "fun" stamps such as Looney Tunes, movie stars, or Dr. Seuss stamps.
• Handwrite the addresses.
• Handwrite your return address without your company name, only first initial and last name.

Once I understood the above process, my mailings were always opened and rarely returned. People actually thanked me for my monthly mailings, as they made my prospects laugh.

Two types of mailings come to mind for this writing. On a monthly basis, send a funny picture postcard (inoffensive) with an appropriate message. One such picture was of a pig wearing cow slippers! My caption read:

"We Offer P.H.A.T. Technology"

Another picture was of a truck sitting in the highest branches of a large tree. The caption for this one read:

"Set Your Goals Higher!"

I used to send this type of mailing once per month for three months in a row to the same contacts. The quantity was kept to four hundred per month. Once all three mailings were received, I would call for an appointment. By this time, I would hear:

> *"Please come in, I'm anxious to meet the person who's been sending these."*

When I walked into the offices, I would see all three mailings hanging on the office walls. Naturally, the monthly mailings continued. In addition to helping me get the appointments, it was a clever and unobtrusive way for me to always keep my name in front of the decision maker. My competition had to hate my strategy.

One client proudly pinned a year's worth of my mailings across her office wall. I was told that she actually brought all of her visitors to see the clever mailings, and even suggested that I was in the wrong field. She told me that my next career ought to be in marketing.

The other system would be to handwrite a legible note asking just one question about their company relating to what you sell. For instance, if you sell HR services, you might write one note a week, each with a different question:

"Are you having difficulty managing benefits?"

"Are you having employee turnover issues?"

"Are you facing administrative challenges and contemplating a change?"

You would include your name and the name of your company at the bottom of the note. After the third note is received, call the prospect to ask one more question and then introduce yourself.

This type of creativity is novel for the prospect. In

addition, I bet many prospects think that if you take that much time to try to gain their attention, you will most likely pay attention to details once inside their company. This point reflects back to the Nice Girl philosophy of showing you care about your prospect's business.

These methods certainly raise the interest level in you and your company to the point of letting you in for the first appointment.

Nice Girl Sales Tips

1. Work on your weaknesses until they become strengths.
2. Become a strong salesperson in all areas.
3. When cold-calling offices, be time-efficient.
4. Look for thriving office parks with full parking lots.
5. Stay away from property management offices.
6. Do research on a company before calling.
7. When speaking live, let the other person know you have visited their website.
8. Create credibility with your first phone call.
9. Pay attention to what you say and eliminate "umms."
10. Ask a question of interest to your prospect, and then introduce yourself while your prospect is formulating an answer to your question.
11. Sharpen your listening skills for information in the voice, such as stress.
12. Call the party by name just as they answer the telephone.
13. Consideration for their time will be greatly appreciated.
14. Duplicate important telephone messages with short email messages.
15. To purposely leave messages during the work week, call

Monday morning and Friday afternoon.

16. When leaving a message, state your phone number *twice*, preferably at the beginning and end of the message.

17. Messages should reflect "*What's in it for them*" to encourage them to call you back.

18. Call decision makers before 8:00 a.m., at noon, and after 5:00 p.m.—when the "gatekeepers" are gone.

19. Call the highest-ranking official possible.

20. Be polite at every turn.

21. Use holiday time to visit offices.

22. Delight the guards and receptionists with candy.

23. At each stage be a value-added resource.

24. Use a clever mailing theme to attract attention.

25. Ask for the appointment.

26. Call when you are feeling upbeat, since the energy comes through on the wires.

27. Move the sales cycle forward.

Final Words of Advice

Whichever task you like the least or dread the most is the one skill you must practice!

Keep leaving a variety of messages to find the most effective; practice cold-calling; and work on conversations with the executive level in organizations.

By practicing your weakest areas, you will strengthen those skills. As you strengthen all aspects of your sales duties, you will become an unbeatable all-around salesperson.

Doing your due diligence, you will find your competition fading away; you will be increasing your ability to put more profit into your sales. And the fun will increase greatly.

11

Strengthen Your Network

If you are employed and have a defined territory, then you know where your clients are and whom to call. However, you may still wish to increase your network and referral base.

The best first step is to determine what your niche market is and acknowledge that not everyone will be a potential client.

Therefore, to maximize your chances, you will want to meet as many prospects as possible in one general location. You will need to determine where your audience is most likely to congregate, and attend those functions. Time is of the essence.

If you already have clients, ask them where they network and to which professional organizations they belong. I did just that, and one client told me about an organization that was a perfect venue for me to find other clients.

Since it was the right fit, at the very first meeting, I met the founder of an organization that helps women become certified as women business owners. After an in-depth conversation with her, I applied for certification for my own business. I believed and it turned out to be true—this process helped to expand my business connections and revenue stream. I was able to network and learn from women far more advanced in their careers. One associate told me, *"You continually advance at lightning speed!"*

Challenge yourself to visit a group where the partici-pants are more advanced in their careers.

Prior to joining a group, ask if you may visit and how many times you may do so as a guest before being required to join. Make a solid determination about whether the group will fit your needs and if you can make a contribution in return.

Through the years, I visited various groups. None of them appeared to be the right fit. Only recently did I find an ener-getic group and one in which many of the businesses comple-ment my own. An added bonus is we have all come to know each other well and many of us are now friends.

Each step you take must be a win-win for everyone in order to proceed.

An article entitled, "Instant Networking" was sent to me. It's a fun variation on the concept of networking. On the spur of the moment, call several associates and ask each of them to call several of their associates for an instant networking party.

Most likely the associates that you would invite are peo-ple you like. Likewise, they will invite associates they like. Statistically the networking group will have a warmer feel to it and you may even find a new friend.

Messaging in a Marketing Sense
Practice what it is you are going to say prior to the next

networking event you attend. Every time you speak, the words you deliver are a marketing message.

Type or write what you say, revise, say out loud, and revise again. Typically, you will want to have a ten-second tag line (for instance—I say, "*I put wind in your sales!*" or *"I hoist your sales!"* for Smooth Sale), a thirty-second commercial, and if you receive keen interest—a two-minute story explaining how you help your clients.

While I have used marketing techniques to get me in the door of accounts, I am not an expert in marketing strategies.

You may wish to consider hiring a marketing consultant. I have heard marketing consultants say that the thirty-second opening should begin with a question pertinent to your niche market. This makes your introduction very personal. For instance, upon meeting you for the first time, and being asked what it is I do, I would ask in turn:

> *"Are you experiencing stormy sales cycles? Are prospects jumping overboard? Do you feel as if business is about to capsize?"*

For me, humor goes a long way and will catch the attention of my audience. At the same time, I demonstrate an understanding of what it is they are experiencing.

Succinctly, I would continue to explain how I solve their sales and business problems, and then give the title of my business, along with one of my tag lines.

You may wish to explore various methods and adapt the best practices of each.

Once you find a group with which to network, you will

be far more successful and eliminate chaos if you follow these Nice Girl guidelines I learned from one such networking group:

- Show a sincere interest in the other person's business.
- Ask who a good lead might be for them and relay yours. (Have you ever met someone who asked this of you? It's a treat!)
- Write a brief recap on the back of their business card for later recall.
- Be generous with advice and referring others to the people you meet. Lend a helping hand. Gradually, the favor will be returned many times over.

As you meet new people, think in terms of how you can help them. They will be surprised by your generosity and will reciprocate whenever possible.

The recap on the back of the business card eliminates confusion when you return to your office. If you attended a successful event and met many people, the odds of remembering the conversations are slim to none.

This method of recapping allows you to contact the interested and interesting parties in an intelligent manner. This is the first step to building credibility.

If you feel shy about approaching new people at events, approach the people who appear to be by themselves, on the sidelines, in a friendly manner. They may be shy, too, and will be very appreciative of your effort. An easy conversation will develop.

As you practice this approach, it will become easier and easier. Over time, I have come to look forward to the networking events, and now feel as if I am going to a party with my friends.

Alliances

While networking, look for businesses with whom you can build new business quickly. For example, a stock broker, financial manager, and real estate investment house may work together to give seminars and assist clients. Their network will grow exponentially.

You may find others who target the same niche market and you will want to exchange leads. Share your knowledge and advice with each other to advance your skills.

The best example I found of forming an alliance was that of an IT person-turned-real estate agent. The agent was new in the field and in a very competitive environment. It was difficult to find clients—until his good friend, a divorce attorney, suggested they exchange leads.

Most people going through a divorce usually sell their home. For the attorney, the exchange became a value-add service and for the agent, a treasure of leads. This alliance was beneficial for all concerned.

Other examples of possible alliances would be real estate agents with mortgage brokers; sales trainers with business coaches and marketing experts. By being creative in forming your alliances, you will be able to penetrate your niche market more quickly.

Speakers

At the networking event, remember to network with the speakers. If they were invited to speak, chances are they have a broad network themselves.

Approach the speaker by saying you found a particular point interesting and want to know more about what they do. You may be able to find a way in which to work together. I have found this to be a very successful strategy.

If you are an entrepreneur, you may want to brainstorm with the speakers to find their secrets of success. Most people find this flattering and are happy to help.

My advice stems from my experience. I met a woman who spoke about her online business and services specifically catering to women. We have kept in touch, she posts many of my newsletters on her website, and I purchased one of her online services. The association became a win-win for both of us.

I exchange links with another who offers a mentoring site. Every other week I send sales tips concerning one sales concept. The site benefits from receiving help from multiple industries and the exposure benefits each contributor.

As you can see, by sharing information with everyone you meet, your network will grow rapidly. The saying goes, "It's not who you know, but who knows you."

Mentors

Utilizing a mentor will help you grow sales and a business exponentially. My definition of a mentor is someone who knows more about a subject matter than you do. By questioning and listening you will take in knowledge far more quickly than if you were to research and practice all on your own.

In your office, talk to the top producers on your team. I remember asking one such person how he was able to meet all his bonus targets even though some seemed so unreachable.

The seasoned salesman showed me how to work numbers backward and forward, literally, on his calculator. He would maximize the compensation plan by throwing in extra equipment "at no charge" to make the bonus numbers. After that, I never missed my bonus targets and my clients were happier than ever.

At another office, my manager had received his training at IBM. You can bet I picked his brain over the course of my employment. I joked with people later on that I was IBM-trained. The most important asset I took away was confidence.

I have found mentoring so valuable in all of my endeavors, that in mid-2006, I will begin the Smooth Sale online and syndicated radio show entitled, "Success Strategies to Catapult Your Business." It may be found at www.women sradio.com. Highly successful women will be interviewed and asked to share their secrets for success. In turn, my audience may model their strategies and succeed more quickly themselves in their own endeavors.

Once again, as you meet people by networking, look for those who can be allies and be of assistance. Learn how they accomplished those tasks you are just beginning to consider.

Attend expos, conferences, meetings, trade shows, listen to CDs, and read books to learn from others. You simply cannot learn everything on your own with a quota or a deadline over your head.

The best mentor of all will be a business coach who takes an interest in your challenges and goals, and who you believe will help you achieve success. Prior to hiring a coach, ask for a complementary session. At the very least, interview several coaches to find how they work and differ from one another. Each business coach will bring his or her own style to the table.

You need to find the one who thinks similarly about business as you and one who will challenge and inspire you to accomplish tasks that you never before imagined yourself doing. By observing businesspeople and salespeople in all industries, you will find mentors in all walks of life. You will learn what *not* to do as well as what to do.

Have you ever received a taped message on the telephone that did not allow for conversation? Have you ever gone into a showroom where a salesman latched on to you and would not stop talking?

We have all seen examples of poor salesmanship. We just have to remember not to copy it. True examples of poor salesmanship:

- A real estate agent discussing another client's finances on his cell phone in front of my husband and I; nothing was confidential.
- A landscape artist, upon being pressed to finish a long past due job for which he was hired, retorted, "I said I 'could' finish the job in four weeks, I did not say I 'would' finish it in four weeks."
- Following your prospect on vacation without being invited.

On the other hand, one time I had the good fortune to visit the French countryside with my husband. There was a little stand in the town of Versailles where an artist displayed small pieces of enameled art on a rack.

The artist spoke no English and our French was so rusty we were silent. However, we did enjoy looking at all of the pieces of art.

The all-time best salesmanship took place with not one word spoken! This artist watched our eye movement. As our eyes rested on a piece we liked, he took it off the rack and placed it on the table below.

Once we had viewed all of the pieces, the artist pointed individually to each piece resting on the table to indicate the question, *"Is that the one we wished to purchase?"*

Taking his cue, we pointed to the one we particularly liked. At that point, the artist pointed to the price on a sign. We gave him the French currency and departed very happy with our purchase and extremely impressed with his power of observation and salesmanship.

Nice Girl Sales Tips

1. Determine your niche.
2. Attend events where your clientele meet.
3. If the group is intimidating, begin with the people by themselves.
4. Demonstrate some knowledge of their business.
5. Take an active interest in the other person's business.
6. Ask questions regarding their challenges.
7. Ask who might be a good lead for them.
8. Be a "matchmaker" by referring business to others.
9. Freely offer suggestions for improvement, resources, and referrals as appropriate.
10. Briefly recap the conversation on the back of their business card.
11. Look for alliances to develop your business more quickly.
12. Speak with the speaker to find a possible connection.
13. Visit networking groups to find if membership is appropriate for you prior to joining.
14. Thank everyone who helps you.

15. When you join a group, become active and offer help.
16. As you become known, referrals begin to come your way.
17. Utilize a mentor to grow business quickly.
18. Listen and observe.

12
Anticipate Your Appointment

Salespeople who try to "wing it" on appointments are usually not invited to return. It's important to realize that a lot of work is required up front before you set foot on the prospect's premises. Doing your homework up front is vital for women breaking into sales. It's a long road to get your stream of income started, so you will want to do everything possible to ensure your success early. By doing the hard work in the beginning, you will harvest far more interest in what you have to offer, and prospects will view you not only as a Nice Girl but as a professional businesswoman too.

If you gained the appointment due to canvassing your territory or through networking, review your notes on the back of the business card. Recall the conversation as to why the prospect may be interested in your services.

After having turned your cold call into a warm call on the telephone, review the conversation in your mind to determine what it was you said that caught the attention of the person on the other end to invite you in for an appointment.

In either of the above scenarios, write notes about what you can say regarding the prospect's interest in meeting with you. What further research do you need to do prior to meeting, and which materials will be appropriate for you to bring? Start planning the potential meeting ahead of time, but be flexible enough to change paths as necessary.

Whether you have an assigned territory or choose where you seek clients, you need to be armed with knowledge. When you are reading, observing, and listening, think in terms of how the subject matters may affect your prospects and/or clients.

For instance, Google is currently in the news for how it does business in China. If you have clients trying to work in China as well, you might ask how Google's experiences will influence their company. Relate current events to your prospect's business as this will demonstrate that you care about their success and you are up to the minute on the news.

Read as much as you can but with the mindset of "how does this affect my clients and prospects?" National news, local news, and business news are the three essential elements on a daily basis. Although you are discussing the news, remain silent on your political and religious viewpoints even if your prospects voice theirs. Many salespeople have been tossed out of accounts for doing just that. You need to focus on intelligently discussing the business-related topics affecting your clientele.

Gala events and promotions will tell you which companies are thriving and who the contacts are at some of these organizations. Advertisements are a good clue as to which companies have money, particularly in slow economic times. It's a known fact that advertising and marketing are the first budgets to be cut when times are bad. If a company is advertising, it signals that they must have other money intact for expenditure or the advertising budget would have been slashed.

Prior to leaving for the appointment, devote time to browsing through the prospect's website one more time to refresh your memory. The information contained on the various pages is priceless.

Nice Girl Sales Tips

On the prospect's website, look for:

1. Repetitive vocabulary
2. Products and services
3. Mission statement
4. Officers of the company
5. Listing of their stock if publicly traded

Notice that repetitive vocabulary is at the top of the list. These words will give you insight as to what is of greatest importance to the company. For example, when I was targeting credit unions, "financial stability" was repeated several times on one website. When the prospect answered her telephone, I said:

> *"I see from your website that financial soundness is of great importance to your company."*

Then I introduced myself and gave the name of my company. The delighted response was:

> *"Oh, yes, that's exactly right!"*

At that time, I was representing a giant conglomerate. My next statement in the form of a question was:

> *"In your mind, do we qualify as a company of financial soundness?"*

The woman on the other end of the phone laughed, having quickly recognized the name of my company and agreed it definitely qualified for the status of financial soundness.

I then focused on setting the appointment.

> *"If so, may I set an appointment with you?"*

My contact on the other end of the phone was very happy to set an appointment with me. By using her company's vocabulary, I appeared to be on the same page and so my prospect could see the benefit in meeting with me.

Just by shifting your technique to incorporate this skill, you will find a noticeable difference in your success at gaining appointments.

If your prospect is at a publicly held company, research what their stock is trading at, as employees like to talk about it—even if the stock is down. Everyone loves to dream about becoming rich. At the same time, read their annual report before an appointment. It will give you great insight into the company.

The more you know about the company ahead of time, the greater the chance for your success. Several things occur when you do the right research, as noted below.

Nice Girl Sales Tips

By doing your homework:

1. Your credibility is greatly increased.
2. It will be very likely your competitors and male counterparts who lack attention to detail and who prefer the quick hit will not take the time to do the research, so it will put you in the lead for earning the business.
3. You will now have enough information to ask intelligent questions.
4. By asking intelligent questions, your credibility will increase further, and your competition will clearly be on the defense.
5. The Nice Girl methodology works time after time.

13
You *Are* the First Presentation

The statistics are shocking! Experts agree that decisions are based upon the following statistics: 7 percent what you say, 38 percent how you say it, and 55 percent how you look.

Clients *want* you to look successful. They want to be able to identify with you and feel good that you are visiting them. The old adage, "People buy from people they like" is true.

Consider this: Have you given money to a salesperson you did not like?

You have to make yourself very likeable.

If you feel uncomfortable in any area of your personal being, seek professional help, such as a business coach or a sales trainer. Lose the extra pounds if it will improve your own self-image. Walk erect and with purposeful strides.

Seek advice from a hair designer, a wardrobe specialist, and a makeup artist. Keep your shoes polished and your suits pressed. Purchase leather accessories and quality pens. It is all these little things that contribute to the image people have of you.

> You must be able to walk into appointments with the
> utmost confidence to conduct business.

By my second year of sales, I knew I needed to make a change. It was nerve-wracking for me to visit with clients.

I registered for the Dale Carnegie Public Speaking Class and paid for it out of my own pocket. The investment was well worthwhile for me to survive and succeed. The first week, when I was asked only to announce my name, I thought I was going to faint.

However, at the final meeting of twelve sessions, I was awarded the grand prize. The class made an enormous difference for my confidence, presentation-giving ability, and storytelling to get my points across. And not only that, the class also contributed greatly to my success in sales. I learned to become a storyteller. This technique made me far more interesting and likeable.

I had come to realize that clients wanted to know about me and my family life. The shared stories of my personal life helped to develop the bond and trust between us. I could entertain clients (and interview for jobs) with stories about our children's choice of universities, our travels, and anything else that came to mind.

As prospects and clients brought up subject matter, I added to the topics with related stories. At this level, they were able to get to know me and feel confident about my credibility. While my clients and I enjoyed sharing stories, I was and still am very sensitive to the Nice Girl philosophy of not monopolizing the conversation. I became proficient at keeping my stories to two minutes or less. The stories were only told if they complemented what my prospects were in the process of telling me and if my story brought a smile to my face.

Rather than following a script, which most trainers suggest, the impromptu nature and candidness of the storytelling serves to show your authentic side. You easily establish commonality and gradually become a confidant for the prospect. This strategy will serve you well to strengthen your relationships with prospects and clients. Storytelling becomes a refreshing way to conduct a business appointment. Promise yourself to throw the script away and be yourself on phone calls and in appointments.

Additionally, the storytelling became so much fun for all of us, it became the strategy that helped secure repeat business. My clients loved having me visit because it was fun!

Storytelling helps build relationships—*and* trust and friendship.

Still, with business in mind, after a digression of mutual interest and fun conversation, I learned the art of how to bring the conversation back to the goal of finding out more information about challenges and needs. It became clear that I was becoming a far more interesting salesperson with whom to communicate. Clients and prospects began to exchange personal information with me. At times, I almost felt as if I were a psychologist. It was the trust building, which became so evident, that helped propel my sales.

Once the relationship is developed, it becomes very easy to uncover the underlying needs for new services and to plan out a long-term strategy together. Percentages for closing greatly increase and repeat business is a natural part of the strategy you are building with your client.

If the strategy is executed properly and you do become the vendor of choice, your client will call you for additional services. As long as you continue to take care of your client, you will cultivate the repeat business.

As businesspeople, we are always striving to hit sales targets but are unsure where next month's income might come from. We tend to worry. By using the Nice Girl philosophy of working to build and strengthen relationships, the sales will come and the worry will subside.

For those of you reading this book who are concerned about speech, voice, delivery of presentation, and just plain old fear, I strongly advise you to research the public speaking training classes available in your area.

Many years had passed since my initial experience with public speaking. The skill had become a passion for me and I knew a brush up would be beneficial. I recently attended a local two-day class to regain confidence in a lost skill, and it was well worth my time. A variety of classes are available for your own skill set and requirements. Opportunities have arisen now where I am asked to give talks about sales and building businesses to a variety of groups utilizing different formats. They include chapters of large organizations, training and business schools, panels, interviews for media, and speaking at conventions. By sharing information freely and speaking confidently, these engagements enable me to promote my sales training services and products. The public speaking skills have come in very handy.

In fact, a chamber of commerce asked me to speak to their membership committee regarding membership retention. This isn't my usual area of expertise. But then I thought of it as a business and mentally walked through the process of what I would do if I were concerned about non-renewals or lost revenue.

I delivered, what was described by the membership director as, *"the best meeting I ever attended."* Public speaking skills are always there to back you up and lend credibility once you have learned them.

More recently, I spent time with a stand-up comedienne to learn how she delivers information to her audiences. I love having fun in whatever I do, and particularly enjoy making people laugh. A week later, I spoke at a women's conference where midway through my talk, on the spur of the moment, I walked into the audience to ask for "recent objections" they may have received to brainstorm a solution. With the video camera on me, I felt like a game show host and the audience loved it! Working with the coach ahead of time, gave me the confidence to pull this strategy off well. The more you increase your knowledge and skills, the more versatile you become and the greater will be your clientele.

> Develop yourself as an expert on your subject matter.

The first way for people to view you as an expert is to volunteer to conduct meetings on your area of expertise. Next, host a public seminar with an ally for further exposure. Once your public speaking takes off, write articles (write in the same manner as you would speak to a friend) and send them to editors of appropriate newspapers, e-zines, and magazines.

Gaining free publicity is something business people should work on in a dedicated manner. Value-wise, publicity is worth far more than advertising. The public realizes you are paying for the advertising and views the ad skeptically. But publicity is a testimonial coming from a third party. It carries far more weight and reaps far greater interest. Last but not least, publicity is free! Publicity will more readily create your persona as an expert than most other avenues.

Nice Girl Sales Tips

1. Convey a professional image in appearance.
2. Utilize professional tools.
3. Walk with confidence and a smile.
4. Do not memorize your talk.
5. Speak about what you are very familiar with.
6. Speak as if you are talking to a good friend.
7. Talk from your heart—show the passion.
8. Add personal anecdotes as appropriate.
9. Adeptly move the conversation back to sales.
10. Seek public speaking help if needed.
11. Be forthright.
12. Ask for questions when you finish speaking.
13. Offer your business card and a follow-up with any audience member interested in speaking with you privately about your services.
14. To gain more business cards, offer a free drawing for a book you wrote, a useful report, or something related to the topic on which you are speaking.

14
Body Language—Another Type of DNA

During the dot-com craze, when everyone was talking about working for a high-tech startup and bragging about the options granted to them, I wanted to be part of the action. I wanted to see for myself what the hype was all about.

The other incentive for moving to high tech, for me, was to completely update my computer and selling skills. I was extremely curious about how it was possible to sell advertising on the Internet.

By this time, I had a number of years of sales experience behind me, as well as repeat business from numerous well-known companies under my belt. Additionally, I had become adept at reading body language.

Over the years, I became acutely aware of body language of prospects and associates. Unusual patterns of gestures and facial expressions of another will affect your outcome. Even Nice Girls have to be streetwise and very aware of others. As you become more observant of these behaviors, you will know instantly whom to avoid. Let me demonstrate by sharing my past experiences.

The manager who willingly interviewed me at the dot-com company seemed nice enough, but there was something suspicious about the way he accented certain statements. He had a habit of quickly twisting his head to his right shoulder as if he embodied an exclamation point. It was truly weird and worrisome. I had seen the exact same behavior previously.

He reminded me of someone, but who?

After the second interview, I became increasingly concerned and spent hours trying to remember whose body language his resembled. With a start, I woke out of a deep sleep in the middle of the night when it hit me who this "manager-to-be" reminded me of.

Several years before, when I was selling networked printers, I was required to bring the color print specialist in to one of my accounts to aid the sale, even though I was very capable. I was already a top producer for the sales organization.

Our manufacturer was very generous with bonus money. Color printers were just beginning to gain popularity, but were still very pricey. A $1,000 bonus reward was being offered for an average of five color units sold that quarter, per sales representative.

The account we were calling on would represent my fifth color unit for the quarter, and I was very excited. This was an account in which I had built steady repeat business over the past year, and they were now ready for color.

However, I made one huge error. I waited until the next morning to put in for the bonus money. While I waited, the color print specialist dashed back to the office and put in for the reward himself, even though it was not his client.

Management (an old boys' network) just shrugged their shoulders and claimed they couldn't do anything to help me. I lost out on the $1,000 bonus money. This color print specialist was the other fellow who used to accent his statements with a twist of his head to his right shoulder.

The similarity between the two men scared me. I just knew I would be in for a rough work experience. I wanted the high-tech experience so badly, I went ahead and accepted on the second interview, although my gut feeling was to not take the job. My head was absolutely throbbing during the entire transition.

Knowing full-well this would be one tough experience, I saved every piece of paper, including a napkin given to me on the interviews stating how much my potential earnings would be, and how my quota would only very gradually rise over the course of the coming year. The napkin displaying expected income figures was a clue to me that it was meant to be tossed, but I knew better. This time, no error was made.

Within three weeks of starting the new job, and to my embarrassment of having to do this so soon, I marched into the HR office. It was embarrassing to have to go to HR on two levels. First, it meant I was unable to resolve the issues myself, and two, it was a new job where I wanted to make my mark, but instead, I would be viewed as a troublemaker. On the other hand, I did not want to be seen as weak and a pushover by my manager. In general, women can be viewed by their male counterparts as an easy target for manipulation. Even Nice Girls need to be prepared to fight back when pushed to the wall.

My goals were now stated to be 500 percent over what had been written out for me on the final interview napkin. As I walked into the HR office, my manager was verbally denying what he had previously told me. He said I was lying. He had a look of terror on his face when he realized I had kept those handwritten notes including the napkin, which I was proudly handing over to the HR manager. We quickly renegotiated to my satisfaction.

Inside sales in the dot-com heyday were conducted swiftly by telephone, and an order would come via fax. I had been waiting only a couple of days for a large order, but it never appeared. As I was reviewing online what was in the queue for all the sales reps, I noticed that the same manager had claimed the awaited sale. He was definitely not a Nice Guy.

This manager had stolen the order off the fax machine and entered it as his own. His body language and behavior matched 100 percent with the color specialist who had stolen the $1,000 bonus money from me.

The manager and I were back in the HR office again. Next, we visited the Vice President's office. Fighting for my rights became a daily routine at this office. Ironically, both the manager and I quit the company within three days of each other. We had been selling advertising on financial sites two months prior to the stock market crash and we both realized there was no point in staying.

Body language and vocabulary are both a part of your inherent DNA.

Nice Girl Sales Tips

1. Conduct yourself professionally at all times.
2. Watch others with a keen eye.
3. Become a student of human behavior.

Observation by Listening and Watching Will Skyrocket Your Sales!

If you are an inside salesperson, you must step up your listening skills tenfold. If you are an outside salesperson, you must listen to what is being said as well as what is *not* being said. You must also be extremely observant of your client's body language. Body language and facial expressions mirror what your client is thinking.

A more pleasant experience reading body language occurred a year prior to the story above. I was still selling networked printers and software in Silicon Valley.

Applying the principles of strategic and top-down selling, I came to know the major players of a high-tech company in San Jose, California. It was clear that the management of the IT department thought our equipment was superior and wanted to purchase equipment for the entire company from me.

The last step was to meet with the purchasing agent, Joel, who was their chief negotiator. The IT manager, Valerie, and I had become friendly by this time. She said to me:

> *"Elinor, although my time is severely limited, I will sit in on the meeting with you because Joel, the purchasing manager, is known for being brutal to vendors."*

I thanked her for her concern and accepted her suggestion to join me on the appointment. By this time, not only did I have years of experience behind me but I also knew that I had done my homework.

Everything the client wanted was in the proposal. It was positioned to accommodate the client's growth and took into account everything shared with me in previous meetings with the various departments. My pricing was very fair, as a huge profit was left out of this one. My goal was to establish a solid business base first and then develop a thriving account where additional money would be made. I wanted the business, and I went for it.

As we reached the door of Joel's office, Valerie whispered to me, "*Good luck,*" with a doubtful tone.

Since I knew the situation ahead of time, I wore my red "power" suit and smiled broadly. Joel greeted me with a grunt of, "*Don't waste my time. Just show me the numbers. I don't want any fluff.*"

Confidently, I flipped the proposal pages to the middle of the package, where the numbers were boldly reflected on the page. This sheet reflected the pricing for the three packages being proposed and the equipment included for each. The last package included much of the IT department's wish list.

As I handed the sheet to Joel, I never took my eyes off of him. The very second his eyes saw the numbers, an immediate smile came over his entire face. Had I not carefully observed him, I would have missed the smile, as it lasted just a split-second.

Instantly, Joel caught himself, changed his expression to a frown, and disagreeably said:

> *"These numbers are not good enough. You will have to redo them."*

I do not recommend you do this in the future, but this is what I said, on the spur of the moment:

> *"I hope you don't play poker. Are you familiar with Kenny Rogers' song, 'The Gambler'?"*
>
> *"From the look on your face, I can see you are out of aces. You've got to know when to hold 'em and know when to fold 'em..."*

As I was saying this to Joel, Valerie was looking at me in horror. I continued:

> *"I saw the initial smile on your face. You know I did a good job for you because I want your business. I could go back and rework the numbers, but quite honestly, there is not much else I can do.*
>
> *I spent considerable time with your associates, making certain to deliver exactly what they want. If I leave now, we will play phone tag, wasting time trying to set another appointment, and then we will have to go through this entire process again.*
>
> *What is your time worth?*
>
> *Let's just do the paperwork now and move forward, to save you time and make your employees happier and more efficient."*

Joel was caught completely off-guard. He asked for my pen and authorized the contract.

Always keep a watchful eye.

Keeping a Watchful Eye

These are some of the negative facial expressions and body language on which to focus: a frown, a raised eyebrow, tightly crossed arms, looking at a watch, looking away and/or coughing as one speaks, contradictions between words and body movement, and looking sideways over the shoulder after a statement is made.

Any time you witness a negative moment, stop and ask if there is a question. You must address all signs of negativity immediately in order to get back onto a positive path.

Positive signs would be a smile, nodding the head up and down, leaning in as you speak, and hearing intelligent questions being asked of you, signaling a buy-in to what you are saying.

Buying signs will include questions of money, deposit, delivery, service, and troubleshooting.

From reading my stories, I am sure you now agree that it is important to keep a watchful eye on everyone with whom you come into contact during selling hours. If you are serious about sales, it is well worth your time to take a class or read a book on the subject of body language.

15
Lobby Your Position!

Nice Girls, pay attention. This is the area where you will easily shine and differentiate yourself from everyone else conducting business as usual. It is always a very good idea to arrive ten minutes early for your appointments. This will give you time, prior to your appointment, to play "detective" by looking for clues. This practice will allow you to observe several areas of the prospect's business and provide you with insight for asking intelligent questions during the appointment.

The Artwork on the Wall

Small offices usually have giant posters decorating the walls since they cannot afford expensive artwork. The posters may focus on teamwork and goal setting, both of which are a good basis for starting the conversation such as, "I see goal setting is of great importance to you." Managers, who walk by the posters every day, seriously forget they are hanging in the hallway. Several have said to me in a surprised and pleased voice, "Yes, how did you know?!"

Larger offices will usually have attractive artwork mounted on their walls. If you like the artwork, say so. Starting the conversation with a compliment is a very nice, friendly way to begin.

Literature

Brochures, press releases, and letters from clients all appear in offices. They will give you additional information. If a piece of literature catches your attention, then by all means mention it at the beginning of the appointment.

Magazines

With a few minutes to spare, pick up one of the industry magazines lying on the table near you. They are filled with information that may be very helpful to you.

For example, I was once impatiently waiting in the lobby for what seemed an unusually long time. My contact, the chief financial officer, was unexpectedly kept in a lengthy meeting.

Usually, if the person I am about to meet is not available within fifteen minutes, I ask to reschedule. The last thing I want to get across is that I have nothing better to do with my time but sit in the lobby or, even worse, that I'm desperate for business.

However, this time, I knew this man had great connections and it was worth my time to wait. Instead of being my normal impatient self, I picked up the magazine next to me entitled, *CFO*.

To begin with, I did not know that sector of corporate America had its own magazine. As I began reading, I found the articles fascinating. By the time I was halfway through the magazine, the CFO came into the lobby to get me. I found myself wanting to read more. I asked his permission to borrow the magazine so that I might finish reading it.

This gesture alone put me high on his credibility scale.

It meant that I was willing to take the time to find out about the challenges he faces. Translating this to the business arena, he began to believe I would take the time to provide a thoughtful solution in regard to his needs and my products.

Reading the information was also an education for me and would be useful in future similar situations. From that point in time onward, I was on high alert in other lobbies to find business title specific magazines.

By the end of our meeting, I was asked for a proposal, which I had not been anticipating. Our meeting had been arranged as introductory, and yet the outcome was potential business—because I showed interest in his arena of the business world.

Awards

Companies proudly display awards they receive. Read what the award was for and who sponsored it. This is a great way to begin a conversation.

Mid-career, I found an award displayed proudly on the counter of a large computer manufacturing company. It turned out to be the Baldrich Award. I had heard of the coveted prize, but wasn't quite certain what was entailed in order to qualify.

After being escorted into my prospect's (Marlene's) office, I mentioned that I had noticed the award displayed on the counter. As good fortune would have it, Marlene was the person in charge of making certain all departments complied with the standards required.

She spoke about the intricacies of meeting all the

requirements. It was a challenging task for her to get everyone in the company to rally behind her and make a team effort to qualify. The description of what went on in that time frame lasted at least forty-five minutes.

By the time Marlene was finished relaying everything, I fully understood the meaning of the award. It also became clear that my company could be seen in the same light for its industry.

My company was ISO-certified for its equipment. Our certification meant that we, too, had to adhere to similar stringent standards. In fact, it was highly unusual for an equipment company of this type to be certified in this manner.

Once Marlene saw the match of high standards between our companies, and saw my interest in her company, I definitely had business forthcoming. While initially I was told, *"We don't need any,"* I came away with an order.

By playing detective in the lobby before the appointment, you increase your chances considerably for walking out with potential business.

Nice Girl Sales Tips

1. Arrive for appointments ten minutes early.
2. Look for clues about the company through the artwork, magazines, and company literature.
3. Include pertinent facts you find in your conversation with the prospect.
4. Point out similarities between your company and that of the prospect.
5. Ask if the similarities are of importance.
6. Proceed down this path for building a partnership.

16
Lessons in What *Not* to Do

Once again, you will escalate your success by observing other salespeople in other industries. While you may read the examples below and say to yourself, *"I would never do anything like that,"* the fact is, every one of these errors is being made daily by someone. Enjoy the stories, but remember them as well.

New Version of "The Tortoise and the Hare"
A software company in Silicon Valley put out a 'Request for Proposal' for new software. Three companies received the RFP.

The president of the software company was very good friends with the president of the largest vendor for software. The friend received the RFP, as did two smaller vendor companies.

There was no doubt that the friend would receive the award for business. However, circumstances change. The RFP was due the Monday morning after the Super Bowl. The friend knew that his company was the vendor of choice. Without further thought, he and his sales team flew across the country to attend the Super Bowl game.

Meanwhile, the two small competing companies worked

the entire weekend. They did not squander a moment watching the game on television.

Of the two small companies, one company went the extra mile by reviewing every minute detail shared in previous meetings by the requesting software company. This vendor gradually came to understand the nuances of the details and further ramifications of all the information presented.

Fine-tuning the details, this small company began to understand how it all fit together with what they had to offer. In other words, they understood the big picture and were able to segment each piece into explicit detail, descriptively explaining how well they would work together in a partnership with the prospect.

Everything the client asked for was put into their proposal. For added measure, the vendor rehearsed with team members about how to present the information at the upcoming Monday morning meeting.

Monday morning finally arrived. The president's friend's company presented first. He and his team members had been drinking and celebrating all weekend. Their presentation was extraordinarily weak and not too coherent.

The second vendor, one of the two smaller companies, presented more professionally. However, they did not quite get all of the details together or lead the prospect into thinking this would be a great alliance between the two companies.

But the third company, the small vendor that paid attention to every detail and rehearsed their proposal, turned heads. To everyone's surprise, this little company won the prospect's very large contract.

Moral of the story: The president of the software company believed that if that small vendor had worked so hard to earn the business, then they certainly would work equally hard to retain the business.

"Too Close for Comfort"

A mainframe computer salesman was very close to making a very large sale. He had become quite friendly with the person making the decision by listening carefully to the prospect.

One day, while the salesman and prospect were out to lunch, the prospect mentioned that he was excited about his upcoming adventure at a baseball Fantasy Camp in Phoenix. He described everything about the camp that excited him. The prospect thoughtfully let the salesman know when he would be away, since they would conduct business upon his return.

The first day at Fantasy Camp, the prospect was astonished to see the salesman walk up to him with a big smile. In the salesman's mind, it was supposed to be a terrific surprise that he was there, so that they could become closer and share the experience.

Instead of the experience being terrific, it became horrific.

The salesman was avoided at every turn and was booted out of his prospect's account.

Moral of the story: Do not cross the delicate boundary between budding friendships at work and private time as this salesman did. He mistakenly invaded his prospect's privacy.

"Dot Your I's and Cross Your T's"

Another mainframe computer salesperson, a top producer at his company, learned a hard lesson about miscommunication.

The client wanted a brand-new computer system that cost $12 million, but it would not be ready for another calendar quarter. The salesman suggested that the client take the $1 million system to tide him over until the bigger, faster system was available. As soon as possible, the new system could be placed on the premises.

The day came when the new system was ready for delivery. The salesman proudly walked in to make the announcement and arrange for delivery. He told the client:

> *"...and when we install the new mainframe, we will remove the old one."*

The client responded:

> *"Wait a minute. You never said anything about removing the first system. Show me where in the contract it states this. We are keeping both systems."*

The computer company had to eat $1 million. The salesman did not make the commission he had hoped for. Luckily, he was at the top of his organization or most likely he would have lost his job.

Moral of the story: Always have someone else look over your contracts for errors and omissions. Legal retainers may also be worth considering.

"Time Management Is Critical"

Once upon a time, I needed to update my kitchen. A new material for countertops was advertised that I had never heard of before. Wanting to make a good decision, I invited the owner of the countertop remodel company to my home to show me what he had.

The owner came and showed off his wares, but I still wasn't convinced. So, he, in turn, invited me to visit his showroom quite a distance from our home. It meant spending a few hours on a Saturday for both my husband and me.

Forty-five minutes later, when we reached the other side of the Bay, the wife of the owner greeted us by asking in an incredulous tone, *"What are you doing here?"*

Upon hearing that we had come to visit the showroom, her face turned white.

The owner of the business did not keep a calendar, nor had he mentioned our appointment to his wife. We had arrived at the exact same time as the Home and Garden Show several cities away. The entire showroom had been dismantled to take to the show. Once again, business was lost.

Moral of the story: Always keep a computerized calendar and a backup calendar (whether paper or in a PDA form) with you for verification of dates.

"Fear Was in His Way"

A bid of about $6 million was in place to install new storage systems for a well-known financial management firm. The technical team, services team, and sales team were working day and night to put together the best proposal ever. This bid was for the teams' current client. They were determined to win.

The salesman in charge, Bob, took the sales job because he thought it would be fast, easy money. He had never sold before, but thought he knew how. He never asked questions, did not find a mentor, and had not talked to the person who had the account before him.

Bob found every excuse he could to work from a remote office. Few in-person sales calls were made. Instead, the technical people were sent to talk to other techies.

Motives and goals were never discussed with the executive-level decision makers. Meetings with the decision makers were avoided at all cost, because Bob did not have the confidence to talk with them.

Bob didn't understand that when a client or prospect asks for information, it is important to ask, *"What is your time frame for receiving this?"*

Bob also did not realize that clients like to be called, visited, and reassured that everything possible is being done to take care of them. He did not know that clients are people who want to develop a comfortable familiarity with their vendors.

The worst error Bob made was to sell from behind his desk, guessing at what the client wanted. He was afraid to visit the client for in-person fact finding. Questions about priority of additional services, budget, and wish list were never addressed.

Bob did not even ask how the vendor decision would be made or which factors weighed most heavily in the decision. In fact, he knew little about this very large account.

The other competing company did not have the best equipment for the job. They bid less equipment for less money knowing full well that if the bid were accepted, they would need to add additional equipment almost immediately. The client understood this tactic.

While the second company had to overcome their equipment inadequacies, their saleswoman called on the top decision makers. She explained her company's proposed strategies and how they could work together. She understood the prospect's challenges and what she needed to do to help solve them.

Fear never stood in her way. It was her company that won the $6 million contract.

After the decision was made, Bob received a scathing email from the client, who asked to meet with the regional director of Bob's company. In addition to the account being lost, the client was angry with the entire company's lack of interest in customer service.

Furthermore, a moratorium was placed on Bob's company for one year. The ex-client issued an edict that no business was to be conducted during this time period with the company Bob used to represent.

Moral of the story: Sales that are relationship-and-solution-based bring a win-win to both sides of the table. Without these three components, a proposal will be meaningless and business lost. The Nice Girl approach wins almost every time!

....
Successful sales are based upon solid relationships, solutions, and win-win for all.
....

You must sell in person, get to know your clients well, and remain in constant communication.

"Would You Believe..."

Our friend, Zach, shared the following story over dinner with my husband and I. Not only is it a juicy story, but it shows how a wannabe salesman, Glen, violated every Nice Guy and Nice Girl rule in the book.

Zach was the lead on a company team established to influence its executives on a major purchase of data storage space.

Zach began:

> *"My story of Glen begins before he changed to the role of salesman to my team. Glen was originally in a technical role where he met another manager of my company. This other manager liked going to Gentleman's clubs, and Glen loved accompanying him there. He had a good thing going because he would write the activities off for both of them as a company expense. Glen also believed that because he had such a close relationship with that manager, he would make a natural salesman. Foolishly, Glen did not realize that the manager was only using him to get into the clubs and drink for free.*
>
> *So Glen jumped at the opportunity to switch to selling to our company instead of remaining in technical support. He quickly realized that I am in charge of a team that has the ear of upper management. Having never sold before, Glen figured it would be far simpler to sell to me than to the executives. He quickly erased his*

> *fear of working with executives by his snap decision.*
> *Glen, focused all of his time on me and my team on a*
> *technical level where he was most comfortable."*
>
> *Zach continued his story. "Meanwhile, Glen missed*
> *his visits to these Gentleman's clubs. Every chance he*
> *got, Glen tried to push my team into going with him*
> *but no one was interested. The men on my team are*
> *married and were offended by the idea of setting foot on*
> *the premises. Glen was oblivious to everyone else. He*
> *only cared about his own desires. I finally couldn't take*
> *the needling any longer. I took it upon myself to 'volun-*
> *teer' to go to one such club in order to get Glen off of our*
> *backs and get our attention back to business."*

Zach's story picked up intensity as did our amazement.

> *"While the two of us were relaxing at the club with*
> *drinks in hand, Glen said to me:*
> *'I'm a little short on cash this month. If you would*
> *pony up $100, we could have a really good time!'"*

(My husband and I were laughing uncontrollably, listening to the recounting of this story.)

Here is the aftermath of that infamous outing:

That was Glen's last visit to the club with an employee.

The client asked that Glen be removed from the
account.

Moral of the story: Momentarily having a good time is
not worth the cost of the job. Listen to your clients!

Nice Girl Sales Tips

1. Learn from others.
2. Meet with the top decision makers.
3. Understand their requirements and goals.
4. Do everything in your power to meet those requirements and goals.
5. Have your prospect's interests in mind before yours.
6. Have management or the legal department look over your contracts.
7. Be respectful of each individual.
8. If you are pursuing business, ignore outside distractions.
9. Sell in person.
10. Establish solid relationships.
11. Salespeople should sell, not technical people. Technical people are excellent sales support people in working on a technical level with prospective clients. However, most techies focus solely on the intricacies of how things work. Executives prefer to know how technical equipment will improve their bottom line, employee morale, and/or cash flow. It is the experienced salespeople who are trained to speak on all of these issues with executive management.
12. Rehearse presentations for powerful delivery.
13. Respect the privacy of others.
14. Keep both a manual and computerized calendar.
15. Do not ask clients or prospects for money; in particular, for something they do not wish to do.
16. Let the client/prospect set the appropriate behavior.

17
If You Want to Know What Your Client Is Thinking, Just Ask!

To be successful at inside sales, you need to have incredible listening skills to make up for not being able to see facial expressions or read body language. The high-tech company was the first company where I accepted an inside sales position. And, you guessed it—there was, once again, no training!

There I was, with limited computer skills, signed up to sell online advertising for financial sites. How was that done? I had no clue. So I did the only logical thing I could think of—I pleaded my case to a potential client.

To make up for stealing the sale off of the fax machine from me, the manager gave me the name of Nancy, the director of advertising at a New York agency. Of course, he failed to tell me that he had had a blowout argument with her and was told to never call again. The cards were stacked against me, but I didn't know it.

I picked up the telephone to call Nancy. When she came on the line, I introduced myself (heard her sigh), and asked if she had five minutes to talk.

My Nice Girl politeness came through, so she agreed. I

then made the following statement, followed by an important question:

> *"I am a seasoned sales professional and have developed a good reputation for taking care of my clients. But I must confess, I have never sold online advertising before.*
>
> *Will you please educate me on what you look for when considering advertising on behalf of your clients?*
>
> *I want to know what will push you over the edge to say, 'Yes, I want to purchase from you.'"*

Nancy's reaction surprised me. She was flattered, and said so. I was taken under her wing so that she could educate me in what advertising agencies want to receive from companies selling to them.

By the time we were done, I had a long laundry list of what she was seeking for her clients. One more time, I repeated back her words for a trial close:

> *"Are you saying that if I provide X, Y, and Z materials for you to review, you will seriously consider them on behalf of your clients?"*

I couldn't believe it would be that easy, and that she would possibly buy from me after I had just asked her to educate me.

She said:

> *"Absolutely. Send your materials over."*

I assured Nancy she would have the materials within twenty-four hours, and thanked her profusely for the knowledge and her time.

Within forty-eight hours after having sent the materials, Nancy conferred with her clients and I had a $10,000 order waiting on the fax machine. Keep in mind, this was during the days of the booming dot-com economy.

Still in disbelief that it was this simple to sell expensive advertising online (as compared to selling copiers and printers where a sale of this size could take up to six months), I called another advertising agency out of the telephone book and asked for their director.

Ode to Vertical Marketing

The quickest way to get started with a business or a new sales territory is to use the concept of *vertical marketing*.

For those of you not familiar with the term, it means that once you find an industry in which you are interested or with which you enjoy conducting business, find other companies to contact within the same industry.

A number of things begin to happen when you proceed with vertical marketing. You automatically bring credibility to the table.

Once you have gotten into the first company, you pick up on some of the industry jargon, challenges, and goals. Providing you were able to develop a good rapport with your previous client, you will then have a very good idea of how your next client would want to be sold. If you have a sales position where it is open territory, you will easily be able to apply the concept of vertical marketing.

As you demonstrate competency in the accounts assigned to you, ask your management if you can cold-call to develop additional business. This is a true Nice Girl strategy to get what you want. No manager or business owner in their right mind will turn down extra business, and believe me, no salesman will ask permission for extra accounts to cold-call. This will be your opportunity to target the business and industry where you think you may have a better opportunity for success.

Once you are granted permission, the most efficient practice will be to establish a long list of high-level contact people and begin calling from the top of the list. Set a goal for the number of new contacts you wish to make every day.

For example, you may decide to tackle ten extra phone calls to digital game developer companies each morning. The important step is to begin your action plan immediately. Using this method will help to fill your pipeline.

The point of all of this is that vertical marketing will get you up and running very quickly. Once you have developed some confidence and success with one type of industry, it will be time to move on to other industries.

The more versatile you become in selling, the more money you will make.

I Chose Advertising Agencies and Directors within Those Agencies

I repeated to the second director of advertising all of the items Nancy required in order to consider advertising on behalf of her clients. This second director was ecstatic. She said:

> *"I have never had a sales rep take the time to familiarize themselves with everything that is necessary to consider purchasing advertising. It's amazing you have the list in its entirety. Send everything over, and I'll purchase from you!"*

Just to be certain, I tried one more agency and asked the same question about necessary materials for them to consider purchasing advertising. The answer was the same.

Remembering the adage:

"If it works, keep doing it."

I performed an Internet search for all advertising agencies in the vicinity. Systematically, I found the name of each director at the agency. I told them of my findings at other agencies, and asked if they worked in the same manner.

Each and every director requested I send over my materials for consideration. Sales were now flowing in.

The only thing standing in the way of an outstanding income for me was the dramatic drop in the stock market. No one wanted to purchase advertising, most of all on financial sites. It was time to move on.

18

Navigate the Sales Cycle Smoothly by Conducting Effective Meetings

My Nice Girl approach is evident to prospects very quickly. The very first question I ask on an appointment, remembering how difficult it was to get there in the first place, is:

> "You are such a busy person. What motivated you to see me today?"

This question provides valuable information: It demonstrates your appreciation of the prospect's time—which they love—and the prospect is now obligated to answer honestly wherein their interest lies.

This eliminates the usual answer:

> "Oh, I was just curious. We really don't need any."

Once the question is answered and your Q&A is complete, you will know how to begin your presentation.

Another very good question for relationship building prior to getting started is to ask:

> *"How long have you been in your position?"*

If the time is less than a year, ask what they did before to get a sense of their history. The answer may include challenges they have faced getting to where they are now. In turn, you can lead the conversation into current challenges.

If they say that they have been in the current position for a long time, you might respond with:

> *"You must have seen a lot of change in that time frame."*

This second statement will also help lead them to sharing information about challenges within the company.

Remember the Vocabulary DNA

• Ask permission to take notes.

• Take notes in the prospect's vocabulary.

• Do *not* translate into your vocabulary.

The vocabulary DNA cannot be refuted, and this tactic eliminates further potential objections.

Ask questions if you do not understand something. It takes confidence to say, *"I do not understand, please explain."* If you do not clarify what is being said, one of the following scenarios will occur, neither of which will help your cause.

1. You will inadvertently get something wrong on the proposal and it will annoy the prospect to the point of not awarding you the sale.

2. If you aren't asking questions, the prospect will think you are not interested and are just after quick money.

The Nice Girl philosophy suggests you begin appointments as a consultant. Allow your prospect to speak first by asking an open-ended question such as:

> *"Please describe the challenges you are facing in detail so I will know if and how I may help you."*

The open-ended questions allow the prospect to begin talking at length.

On every new appointment, you have two goals. The first is to dig deep enough to find where money and productivity are being lost. The second goal is to find three to five buy-ins and the third goal is to find three to five needs. Buy-ins are agreements stated by your prospect such as, *"Yes, service is more important than price."* Another method for gaining agreement is to ask questions with the following lead-in phrases:

- Isn't it...
- Wouldn't it...
- Couldn't it...
- Shouldn't it...
- If I could, would you...

For example:

- *"Isn't it true that speed is very important?"*
- *"Would you prefer it if your vendor offered Olympic-sized swimming pools?"*
- *"If I could throw in a year's supply of ballpoint pens, would you be interested?"*

By obtaining the answer *"Yes"* from these questions, sprinkled throughout the conversation, (you wouldn't ask them rapid-fire all in a row), your prospect gradually becomes drawn to you because the conversation has become very positive. Your prospect is beginning to believe you truly do want to help and are seeking the best solutions possible for them.

By asking these questions, you will soon have the three to five buy-in agreements needed. These agreements will also make the prospect more amenable to admitting their three to five needs when it is your turn to make your presentation and ask more questions.

Be aware that only one need will not produce a sale. Instead, the prospect will sit on the fence and wait. To be truly motivated to make a costly change, the prospect must have three to five needs. The prospect must believe you are the one who will be able to satisfy the needs and help their business grow. By questioning and digging, you will find the necessary information to advance to the proposal stage.

But first there is more work to be done. Resuming the question-and-answer period, your prospect's response may be:

> *"I'm losing money because work isn't processed quickly enough."*

Follow-up questions to this might be:
- *"Are you losing clients because the turnaround is too slow?"*
- *"Is morale low because of the work frustrations?"*
- *"Are you experiencing turnover because of the low morale?"*
- *"How much is it costing you to rehire, train, and start new benefits?"*

I have heard a few people say that the overall cost of rehiring and retraining is as much as $125,000 per person.

- *"How much do you think it will cost if you do nothing to improve the system?"*

Do you see how one statement can lead to many other pertinent questions? Do you also see how one statement will lead to justification to acquire new services?

This last question will get the prospect to think of the cost of doing nothing—which leads to loss of business—versus the cost of improving the processing system, leading to building business.

Once you elevate yourself from the position of salesperson to the level of consultant, these questions will all be answered honestly. The questions must be asked diplomatically for the prospect to be able to see your desire to help resolve the situation.

As the answers pour forth, ask related and specific questions to truly understand the ramifications and the havoc that may be playing on the rest of their business.

Finally, you will want to know how your two top competitors (not necessarily the biggest and the best, but the ones you come across most often) perform or implement a similar service. Do not bad-mouth your competition, but instead, share your knowledge of them and how they operate. Know how to spin your difference in a favorable light. Then ask your prospect which method is preferred. This will bring you tremendous buy-in to what you have to offer—as long as you are 100 percent truthful.

For instance, prospect John is considering either the purchase of a copier or relying strictly on a copier service. If you were the salesperson selling the copier, you might ask:

> *"Are your projects delivered to you on time, 100 percent of the time?"* and, *"Do your projects arrive correctly formatted 100 percent of the time?"*

My experience has been that upon being asked these questions, people laughed and then recalled the nightmare experiences of having to turn projects in late and enduring the consequences.

However, when selling document services, I would ask prospects:

> *"Does your technician always show up promptly? Have you ever had projects delayed due to the equipment being down? How is service during the winter? Is service turnaround particularly bad due to the flu season and car accidents caused by hard rains?"*

As I painted pictures of delays and time wasted waiting for the copiers to be fixed, I could see the distress in their faces. They were ready to talk about having a service in place as an option.

The questions and the integrity you bring to the meeting will be appreciated as they show you are paying attention, and that you are truly interested in solving the prospect's problems. Once your prospect determines you truly care and will help solve their issues, your status as consultant will change to that of partner. You will be able to delve into the heart of the matter that is troubling your prospect to develop a win-win solution.

What you are selling is not so much the service or product itself, but rather you are selling yourself, service, and value. Once your prospect realizes the value you bring to the table, the price objection will most often disappear. You will still need to ask what their budget is. An added strategy is to ask:

> *"If money were not an issue, what would your wish list look like?"*

Prospects love that question as it allows them to day-dream if only for a minute. Most salesmen feel they are too busy to ask those types of questions so they don't. By the time all proposals are received, yours will be eagerly read. Your proposal will definitely stand out and you will be remembered as the Nice Girl.

My clients always ask if they should lower their pricing when they hear objections to how expensive they are. The simple answer is no. It shows a lack of confidence in yourself and in your business. The longer answer is that these businesspeople considering lowering their prices have overlooked vital information, such as budget and time and cost justification in their question-and-answer period.

When selling your services you must always find a time and cost justification for the changeover. Other questions would include:

> *"Have you considered what will be the cost of not moving forward?" "Are you losing clients, profits, or employees—what is that costing?" "How much more business do you believe you will acquire by moving over to our service?"*

Your prospects have the same revenue issues you do. They, too, are dependent upon selling with profit. If you are able to discuss their revenue challenges and goals, peer-to-peer, you will easily transition to partner status.

> You need to be able to speak to your prospect's bottom line. To sum up, the Nice Girl approach reveals sincerity and integrity, and builds heavily upon value.

Once all of your questioning is complete, it now becomes your turn to take the floor. The moment I begin to speak, I mention price. This is where I differ from most salespeople. In fact, at one office, my male counterparts, including management, had a loud discussion in the hallway with me saying I was "nuts" to bring up price right at the beginning of a conversation. They saw no correlation between my doing so and being the top producer in the office! The first words I utter are:

> *"My company is not the cheapest on the market. If price is your first and only consideration, then we are not the company for you. On the other hand, I do believe we have an excellent solution for your situation, and I will make certain excellent service is available to you.*
>
> *Are you most concerned about price, or are you looking for a complete solution to your problem(s)?"*

Most people shudder at the thought of mentioning price up front. My Nice Girl thinking is that hiding price until the end of an appointment, or worse yet, not divulging cost until presentation of your proposal, is less than ethical. In my opinion, it weeds out prospects who are not truly interested, and eliminates price objections when it comes to the proposal stage of the sales cycle.

From the brief and forthright statements above, you have set the stage for building in numerous benefits: You are now able to build in a reasonable profit as long as you are within the guidelines of what the prospect requested and have their budget in mind.

You now have your first agreement that the complete solution is more important than price alone.

> By mentioning price up-front, your prospects will appreciate the honesty. This Nice Girl approach will set you apart from the competition.

Clients want to believe they have purchased the best they could afford. By placing a higher value (within reason) on your service or product, it will appear to be superior than if you offered it at a discount rate.

Think about one of your favorite department stores. When you see designer clothing next to the less expensive clothing, don't you sometimes wish you had the extra dollars to spare for the designer goods?

This is the same concept. You want to present ultimate value to build in a reasonable profit. You also want to sell with the attitude, *"you get what you pay for."* By adding value to the mix throughout the sales cycle, you will be able to accomplish the goal of adding in profit.

For instance, I used to tell potential clients that over

time, a copier will need servicing. When that occurs, they should call the 800 number to get into the queue for service. However, if they are experiencing a major problem, they should also call me personally, and I would do everything in my power to get the problem resolved immediately.

This one Nice Girl offer alone made a huge difference. Not too many salespeople would put themselves on the line like that. Clients found me very believable and I always followed through.

> Follow-through is where 90 percent of the competition fails.

Most salespeople are looking for the "easy" clients. They don't want to go out on a limb for them, jump through hoops, or make a couple of extra calls. They simply want the order with little or no effort. Buyers are too savvy today to put up with pure self-interest on the part of the vendor.

What I find comical is that these same salespeople will spend years perfecting their follow-through on the golf course. But where their income is concerned, they give follow-through very little regard. By concentrating on perfecting your follow-through in the sales cycle, you will increase your income substantially.

Never, ever make a promise that you won't or can't keep. Word will get around that you are not true to your word and your business will decline.

When writing proposals, you must keep in mind that people do not like to read. In particular, people do not like to read "fluff." Change your creative style on proposals to that of sticking with only the facts. This technique is especially important if you have captured the prospect's vocabulary. Your proposal will come across as highly credible whereas most others will not.

Answer Strategy

Your prospect will be asking you questions in a give-and-take manner between your questions. It is very important to give full attention to the question being posed. I say this because I have asked questions of two different business types and was the recipient of two exasperating experiences.

The first person to whom I posed a question, in regard to changing over to his service, gave me a forty-five-minute answer. It was very difficult to sit through his monologue. By the time he finished, my response was:

> *"That was a fascinating answer, but did not correspond with my question."*

Trust me; I was fearful of another forty-five-minute answer.

His lack of taking the time to understand my question first, and then lack of courtesy to answer succinctly, led me to believe he was more interested in his own success than in my situation. He subsequently lost the business.

The second situation took place at an upscale hardware store where I asked the sales representative for advice on new cleaning agents. Her answer, to my horror, was:

> *"You need more elbow grease. Get your grandchildren to help!"*

Her answer made me feel very old. The first thing I did when I returned home was look in the mirror. She was lucky I was on the receiving end. If this remark was said to another woman, someone who wasn't able to have children of her own, or didn't want children, that woman could have been very angry.

Always think before you speak; a brief pause will help. And, remember, if a prospect asks a question of you that you cannot answer, it takes confidence and a Nice Girl attitude to say:

> *"I don't know, but I will have the answer to you within twenty-four hours."*

Once again, honesty is appreciated and will help build credibility and trust. Just make certain to follow up in that time frame. If an expert or higher up official from your office will lend credibility to the advancement of the sale, offer to bring her in. But make certain he or she will not bore the prospect to a no-sale status.

Nice Girl Sales Tips
1. Be fully present when asked a question.
2. Take a moment to comprehend the question and formulate an inoffensive answer.
3. Keep your answer short.

Questioning Strategy: Developing Needs and Wants

As your clients begin to trust you and relay what is on their minds, you will respond directly to their statements. As mentioned before, clarify anything you do not fully understand.

If a statement made by your prospect can take a direction of two or more paths, ask which path would be more important. You will want to phrase your question so that the prospect will choose the path that your company can best service.

For instance, I tried for a very short period of time to sell long-term care insurance. I didn't last long, because I found the subject matter depressing—not a good match for making sales! Nevertheless, there was one issue that my company and its competitors needed to address to lead the prospects down the right path in order to make the sale.

The subject matter was what to do when your loved one requires use of the insurance and a private nurse for an immediate health care issue.

The competitors said:

> *"With our company, you can call whomever you like to care for your spouse. That way you will be 100 percent comfortable with the person who comes into your home."*

Knowing this was a big issue, I raised it first, and asked:

> *"Should your spouse take ill, will you know who in your community is among the best of health care professionals? Would you know who to hire and whom you could trust?*
>
> *Our company will send out a specialist to determine who in your community will best fit your needs in such a stressful time. Will that be of importance to you?"*

Not having run into someone familiar with the medical community, everyone I encountered said, yes, it would be important to them to have a specialist visit first. The way my company handled the situation is what they would want.

The question separated my company from its competitors and cleared the way to be seriously considered as the prospect's vendor.

Specific Questions to Ask

In order to develop a valid proposal, these are the specific questions that must be asked:

- What is your budget?
- What do you estimate the cost of not moving forward to be?
- How will your decision be based?
- Can you prioritize those criteria?
- If you had a wish list what would it look like?
- Is there anything you can think of that would push you over the edge to say "yes"?
- Which other vendors are you considering?
- What are you looking for in a vendor?
- Does my company sound like one with which you would like to work?

- I will be your representative. Will you be happy working with me?
- What is your time frame for the changeover?

Why would I suggest you ask these particular questions? Let's examine each question in order.

Budget

Without knowing the ballpark amount your prospect has in mind, your proposal will not be valid. You must discuss this in depth and not be afraid of the question.

If your prospect states a very low amount in the budget and it sounds ridiculous, you will need to pinpoint exactly which services or products the company truly needs. It will then be your job to explain the details of putting the requirements together and gain agreement that there will be room in their budget to accomplish what they are seeking.

Not Moving Forward

Remind your prospect of all the problems shared with you and the implications for slowed business or loss of business. If employee turnover has become an issue, remind your prospect of the high cost of retraining. This will determine whether or not your prospect is serious about moving forward.

Basis of Decision

This question will determine if you will be a serious contender for the business. You will now know if you will be able to meet their requirements.

Sometimes it is necessary to say, *"I'm sorry we cannot do that,"* and walk away. Most of the time, however, the answer will allow you to zero in on what you need to say next and how to write the proposal.

Prioritization of Criteria

You will now know exactly what is most important and where your focus should be for further meetings and for your proposal.

Wish List

Occasionally, your prospect will open up and tell you all about the company and personal goals. This prospect will be only too glad to share with you their wish list and pinpoint which extras to put into your Proposal. You will have to choose one of two paths for this section. One, create a more expensive package with extra profit for yourself, or two, squeeze as much of the wish list in as possible as a bonus for your prospect in order to secure extra business.

Over the Edge

This takes the previous two questions a step further. prospects are now sensing you truly want to earn their business and that you are obviously trying very hard to please. They may either laugh and say, *"No, just bring me a good proposal,"* or they will actually confide the secret if there is one. Either way, you are now in their very good graces by asking pinpointed questions for clarity.

Other Vendors
Most prospects will tell you who else they are considering, while some will be coy and tell you:

> *"You are the first,"*
> *"You called me and got me off guard," or*
> *"I haven't yet considered who else to call."*

These three responses are fine. However, if you hear, *"You are the only vendor I'm considering,"* do not trust the response. In my experience, it has almost always been untrue.

The best case will be if they tell you who the other competing vendors are, so that you will be able to effectively sell the differences between all of you. Otherwise, you will have to be a perfectionist with attention to every single detail and proceed as if they are considering your top competitors.

Desires for a Vendor
Once again, this question will allow you to determine if your company can meet the requests of your prospect. If the requirements are valid, you know you are in the game.

Working with Me
This is one of my favorite questions. It rocks the prospect back on their heels, as it requires a truthful answer. It catches them off guard and so, by watching their facial expression and body language, you will know instantly whether you have a decent chance of succeeding. This is truly a Nice Girl strategy and the question is asked with innocence. I do not

believe any of the men I worked with over the years would ever have asked this question. I truly believe their egos could not have handled a "no."

Normally, by this time, when they are telling you, *"Yes, I would like to work with you,"* your chances for succeeding are far greater than those of your competitors. However, the deal is not done. You still have to compose a very thoughtful proposal to win the business.

Time Frame
You need to know, for your own sake, and for the management of your company, when your prospect truly plans to make a change. You need this information for forecasting and for scheduling the work ahead of you.

Additional questions to ask, along with time frame, are:
• When is the deadline for the proposals?
• How much notice will you give me between choosing me and wanting the new service?

Asking the second question regarding notification to implement the new service paints a positive picture of working with you in the future because it shows that you are concerned about every detail.

If the transition period is too short a time, this is when you must tell them what it will take on your part for the switch to happen. As long as everything is clarified up-front, most prospects will accept what you say.

As your client unloads all of his/her likes, dislikes, needs, wants, and wishes, do *not* translate the information into your vocabulary. Instead, accurately write down, in their own words, what is being said, as they are saying it.

Transcribe as would be done in a court of law. Why?

Again, remember the vocabulary DNA—it cannot be refuted, and this tactic eliminates further potential objections. This step is so important, it is worth repeating and rereading.

Just as with the initial questioning, if you do not understand something that is said, clarify. Repeat back the words that you do not understand exactly as they were told to you. Ask for an explanation. Your client will appreciate the interest and the desire to get the information correct.

Once again, you have put yourself ahead of the competition by giving 100 percent of your attention to the client. This is extremely important, as you are going to put all of the client's words back into a proposal.

At the end of your meeting, recap the highlights of the discussion with your prospect. Reiterate the remaining steps necessary before presenting your proposal. Ask if there are any remaining questions. Do your best to set a return appointment before you leave the premises.

Providing you listened carefully, took notes in your prospect's own words, and transferred them into a proposal, there is very little room to argue with the final proposal. This is similar to a chess move. You will be able to say, under your breath, *"Checkmate!"*

You are now ready to put the prospect's words into a proposal.

Nice Girl Sales Tips

1. Ask your prospect for the information you need.
2. Prospects and clients like to educate their vendors.
3. Make the sale a win-win for all concerned.

4. Ask your prospects why they took the time to see you.
5. Let the prospect speak first.
6. Find three to five agreements.
7. Use tie-down questions to get the agreements.
8. Find three to five needs.
9. Look for justification in lost money and time to switch over to your service.
10. Dig deep on the needs.
11. Take notes in the prospect's words.
12. Incorporate the must-ask questions into your discussion.
13. Clarify anything you do not understand.
14. After each section of concern, recap the highlights of the discussion.
15. When it is your turn to present, mention price up front to eliminate a price objection later
16. Sell value.
17. Become familiar with your competitors' strategies.
18. Sell the difference between you and your competitors.
19. Lead the prospect down the path of choosing which method is of greater importance.
20. Ask if they will be comfortable doing business with your company.
21. Verify that they will want to work with you as their representative.
22. Recap highlights.
23. Obtain their budget.
24. Determine priorities for decision making.
25. Ask for a wish list.
26. Get their time frame for the transition.
27. Set a return appointment.

19
Expand Your Client's Horizon

Writing a proposal the first few times can be very time-consuming and overwhelming. There are several ways to help if this is a fairly new process for you:

- Follow the order of your questions.
- Schedule several evenings of quiet to write the proposal.
- Have a more experienced person read the complete draft for suggestions, inclusiveness, and accuracy.

The most difficult part is getting started. Begin by entering into your computer all of your notes exactly as you took them in your meetings. Remember, people do not like to take time away from work to read lengthy documents. Keep your proposal simple, factual, and to the point.

In anticipation of the need to prepare a proposal, ask counterparts if you can look at proposals they have developed. Adapt one to your style and make it your own. Your authentic style will shine through on the proposal and lend credibility. All proposals should be logical and clearly demonstrate your understanding of the prospect's business. Doing so will greatly increase your prospect's perception of your credibility. Below is a sample of how one proposal might appear.

Section Headings

For proposal writing, develop section headings:

> - *Purpose for Our Meeting*
> - *Issues Discussed*
> - *Time and Revenue Loss*
> - *Personal and Corporate Goals*
> - *Needs*
> - *Wish List*
> - *Packages with Pricing*
> - *Reasoning for Each Package (Justification)*
> - *Timeline and Transition*
> - *Expiration Date*
> - *Contract*

Proposal Example
I. Purpose for Our Meeting

A short, introductory paragraph will describe the basis of your conversations and why you were there in the first place. "Currently, the computers throughout XYZ Company are very slow and are creating a number of problems, leading to lost business. It is of utmost importance to recover and to begin building revenue once again."

Do you see how writing the proposal in the prospect's words is critical? An introductory paragraph, similar to the one above, will be refuted if the prospect does not recognize the verbiage. If the vocabulary is recognized, your prospect will be uncomfortable, but will urge you to move on to find out how they can solve the issues.

II. Issues Discussed
Under each subheading, number each statement as follows:
1. Slow computers
2. Clients not receiving work on time
3. Lost business

III. Time and Revenue Loss
1. Employee morale low
2. Employees needing to work longer hours for the same pay
3. Employee turnover
4. Costly training of new hires and ramp-up time
5. Frustrated clients are leaving
6. Profit margins dwindling
7. Shareholders not happy
8. Bad press
9. Working hard to earn a promotion, but not likely to happen with leakage of employees and revenue

Based upon the conversations with your prospect and your careful notes, fill in as much factual information as you possibly can under each section.

IV. Personal and Corporate Goals
1. Desire a six-month vacation in Europe
2. Earn recognition by the board as doing an outstanding job steering the company
3. Turn the leakage of employees and clients around to long-term status
4. Reap referrals by all
5. Earn the industry standard award

V. Needs

1. Faster computers
2. Increased memory
3. DVD capability
4. Improved morale
5. Regain and build business

Providing you address all these areas: wants and needs; creativity and value-add solutions; and budget, your closing percentages should rapidly increase.

Next, you will address the wish list. In the rare occurrence where a prospect does not have such a list, you can add a section entitled "Extras."

Only use this heading if you can think of valid add-ons to enhance what is being asked for. List the extras underneath with a one sentence explanation about how they relate to the areas already mentioned.

VI. Wish List

1. Projection system
2. Six extra computers for potential new employees
3. Upgraded software

Here comes the fun part of devising two or three packages for the prospect. If your package is complicated (a long list of items), only include two choices. Providing your solution is straightforward and easy to comprehend, offer three choices.

The first package will reflect exactly what the prospect requested up-front. The second choice will have some or all of the wish list included. The third selection will incorporate extras that you determine will benefit their business.

This section may be entitled "Package Description."

List everything that is included in each package. Provide subheadings such as Package #1 so that each package is easily identified.

For ease of reading, columns work best for easy comparison by your prospect.

VII. Packages with Pricing

Package #1	Package #2	Package #3
12 Computers	12 Computers	18 Computers
Laptop 2000	Laptop 2004	Laptop 2005
Pentium 4	Pentium 4	Pentium 5
External CD	Internal CD	Int. DVD/CD
2 MHz	2 MHz	3 MHz
Software	Software	Software
---	Projection	Projection
---	---	Ergonomic Features
Warranty: 30 Days	90 Days	2 Years
$26,000	$29,500	$42,500

(Please note, these are fictional computers and prices, and are shown only for layout purposes of the proposal.)

By providing a side-by-side comparison, your prospect will be able to easily zero in on the favored package. Notice, after the last conversation, you thought to include a longer warranty period and ergonomic features.

The buying decision will actively be taking place at this point.

Once you know what you are proposing, you begin to start adding the dollar value for each line item. The prospect will be evaluating the total dollar cost versus value-add services.

VIII. Reasoning for Each Package (Justification)
Package #1
The first package should be under the stated budget. You may begin presenting this package in a style similar to:

> *"You shared that your budget is a maximum of $27,000. All of the software and hardware components of this system will help your business and your employees, considering anticipated growth for the next two years."*

Package #2
The second package may be at the stated budget or—within reason—over budget. However, this option must reflect sound business reasons for going over budget. At this point, you must keep in mind the prospect's individual goals as well as the corporate goals. Your conversation may sound like this:

> *"Although your stated maximum budget is $27,000, you may wish to consider a small increase, to $29,500. For the extra $2,500, you and your company will receive a newer computer model, an internal CD drive, a projection system, and a longer warranty.*
>
> *The newer technology, convenience, and longer protection may well be worth going over your budget a little. The decision is yours."*

Package #3

The third package is to be presented as "the best of all worlds," or "for down the road, when business takes off." It is on your proposal only to tempt the prospect. You may teasingly say:

> *"This third package is presented to you as the best of all worlds. It incorporates your entire wish list. Additionally, I researched all of the latest software and found that the type listed will benefit you the most.*
>
> *Now I know this is a 'reach for the moon' type of package, but I thought it might be worthwhile to put down on paper so you can see what is available and what is possible."*

Note that as you read the descriptions of packages two and three, there are subdued words of encouragement for moving forward with either of these.

The Nice Girl strategy is to come across as being happy with a sale, and so whichever package is chosen is fine with you. Assure your client that they will receive the same outstanding service no matter which they choose.

You will be surprised on occasion when the third option is chosen. You may hear:

> *"Oh, what the heck, we know we need it, let's just do it now. It will save a lot of time in the long run."*

I have even heard:

> *"I'll just take the extra money from another budget."*

These last three sentences will never be shared with you before the proposal. They come as rewards when you have done what is considered an outstanding job.

Describe in separate paragraphs how and why you put each package together. Relate the development of the package process back to the information shared in your meetings. Always be sure to match your ideas with your client's vocabulary to minimize objections.

IX. Timeline and Transition

Nice girls understand their prospects will want any transition to be painless. Outline, in very simple terms, everything that will transpire in order for your prospect to take advantage of what you are offering.

Briefly describe how the timeline and transition will be handled, and the time allotted for completion. Make the changeover sound effortless with the least amount of disruption. But above all, be honest.

At this very moment, your prospect is very seriously considering your service. You do not want the prospect thinking, *"Wow, this is complicated. What have I gotten myself into?"* Don't ever fool yourself into thinking, *"They signed, I don't have to work so hard any more."* I have seen many sales go off the road and crash by this attitude of other salespeople.

If you are selling a service where a transition is not required (e. g., moving the old service out first), write a brief description of how the company will acquire your service, the time it will take to do so, and when your company will best be able to see it implemented.

X. Expiration Date

It is very important to include an expiration date underneath the listing of the packages. You will have to determine what is reasonable within your own company guidelines.

You do not want your prospect to be able to *"think about it"* for too long, or nothing will be done. In fact, you want your proposal to be so attractive your new client will not have to think about it at all. Instead, due to your attractive and thoughtful proposal, your new client will want to authorize the sale at the time of discussion.

XI. Contract

Finally, after the expiration date, include a contract. Fill out as much of the information as possible beforehand. Highlight all areas where the client will need to authorize.

Have a separate blank contract in your briefcase, in case you are hit with a surprise and changes need to be made. If you are new, errors may be made and you will be glad you had the extra contract on hand.

XII. Final Additions

If you are selling a service or product that has a brochure, by all means attach it to the end of the proposal. Make the proposal look as professional and personalized as possible. For an extra Nice Girl touch, take a screenshot of your prospect's logo online. For those of you not familiar with the term, bring up the company website on your computer. Place your cursor on the company logo. At the same time, press three keys: Control, Alt, and Print Screen. Paste what you just copied into Paint or another editing package and highlight the area you want. You can now copy and paste the logo into your proposal and copy the company mission statement below it. Not too many salespeople go to all this trouble. Once again, your effort will be appreciated and make a lasting impression.

Rather than just stapling sheets of paper together, acquire a small binder or attractive folder in which to put the paperwork. Always demonstrate value in everything you do.

A day or two before the final presentation call your prospect and say something similar to:

> *"I have finished putting together the proposal for you, and I know you will be excited about the final result. I am calling to get the final number of people who will be sitting in on the meeting so I can prepare enough copies of the proposal for everyone."*

The prospect will now be very curious as to what you have put together. The prospect will also be appreciative of your consideration to have a copy of the proposal for each attendee.

The night before the final appointment reread your proposal. Double-check that you have all of the paperwork assembled that will be required. Also have a couple of good-looking pens to take to the appointment. Practice your Nice

Girl smile, and get plenty of sleep!

Nice Girl Sales Tips

1. Set quiet time aside for writing.
2. Find a proposal format that will work well for you.
3. Capture the prospect's words in the proposal.
4. Offer two or three packages depending upon the complexity.
5. Include a timeline, expiration date, brochures, and the contract.
6. Add wish list or extras, as the case may be.
7. Keep blank contracts in your briefcase for possible changes.
8. Have someone more experienced review the documents.
9. Review the proposal yourself the day before your presentation.
10. Call the prospect saying you have finished and that they will be delighted with the results.
11. Make enough copies of the proposal for each person in attendance.
12. Give the proposal a professional presentation.
13. Acquire a few quality pens for finalizing the contract.
14. Rehearse the delivery.
15. Practice smiling.

20
How to Deliver Your Proposal

Whenever possible, the Nice Girl strategy is to deliver your proposals in person. Clients have confided to me that their proposals often die on the vine. After probing, I found that the dead proposals had been faxed to the prospect.

Once again, put yourself in the shoes of the prospect. Do you have jargon in the proposal that will not be understood? Is the logic of the proposal clear, or is it difficult to follow?

How will questions be answered? Do you really think your prospect will take the time to call you to ask questions?

Most importantly, what do you think your prospect is thinking when they receive your faxed proposal? Assuming you are within driving range, is the prospect thinking you are too lazy to come over, or that you think your time is more important than theirs?

Remember, too, that faxed materials lose a generation of quality. What kind of presentation and impression will this make?

Usually faxed proposals appear to be "boilerplate." This can lead to the conclusion that the person faxing the proposal is only interested in collecting the commission and does not want to work with the client to find a solution to earn the business.

The other downside of not delivering a proposal in person is that the salesperson will miss out on important body language and facial expressions that will occur during the reading of a proposal. That is when miscommunication can be restated, facts clarified, and the proposal saved.

It is far better to personally hand a copy of the proposal to each attendee and say, *"Thank you."*

You are in charge of this meeting and so it is up to you to call the shots. The very first question to ask before anything else takes place, is:

> *"Has anything changed since we last met?"*

It would make no sense to spend an hour delivering your proposal when all the while the parties know that budgets have been put on hold, or that some other circumstance will prevent you from moving forward.

This also gives you the opportunity to make adjustments if there were minor changes within your prospect's company. The possibility also exists that your prospect's company has just announced an acquisition or merger. For all of these reasons, you must ask the question, *"Has anything changed?"*

If nothing has changed, you now have the green light to proceed. The very next question to ask is:

> *"Are there any questions before we proceed?"*

If there are questions, only answer the questions that are asked. Do *not* volunteer additional information at this stage. It will only open a hornet's nest. After it appears that all questions are answered, ask the next question:

> *"Are you ready to proceed?"*

This second question creates anticipation and generates a buy-in, signaling that they are interested in hearing what you are about to tell them. At this point, your prospect is cautiously optimistic.

You now have the floor. This is your show. Explain how you will proceed through the proposal and then follow the course of the actions laid out.

You must read the proposal line by line. Quickly scan every sentence and then speak each one with enthusiasm while watching the faces of everyone in attendance.

The very second you see an eyebrow raised, a squint of an eye, someone leaning back or crossing their arms—STOP. Ask if there are any questions. Once again, only address the questions at hand and then move on.

If everyone looks perfectly content, only ask for questions at the end of each section. Once again, only answer the questions asked. If for some reason a question is asked for which you do not know the answer, simply respond:

> *"That is a valid question. I do not have the answer right now, but will get it for you immediately. If the answer I receive is negative, will the process be delayed or will it be a showstopper?"*

As hard as this may be on you, it will be harder if you don't know and do not ask. If you continue assuming everything is okay and you move forward to predict and count on the close of the sale, only to have it postponed at a later point, this course of action will not sit well with your management. In fact, it will cause a chaotic situation in the office.

Everything must be out in the open at this point. Honesty is truly the best policy for impending sales.

My clients have all appreciated my directness and complete openness about circumstances. I don't have time to play games and neither do they. Avoidance is not a strategy and will not get you to your goal. Management loved that I asked the hard questions because it enabled me to keep them up-to-date by the minute on each account. I always knew the next step and where I was headed with the account. Clients and management alike showed their appreciation for my honesty and willingness to work with them by rewarding me with business and bonuses.

If you promise your prospect an answer within twenty-four hours, be certain to deliver the answer within the promised time frame. Should you determine it will take thirty-six hours to find the answer, then call long before the initial twenty-four hours come and go.

Be straightforward and tell the prospect it will take longer than expected, but you will keep them apprised and will call back as soon as you have the answer. Give another estimate for when you might have the information. This time, give a longer deadline than you believe it will actually be.

Oddly enough, clients remember if you promise something by a certain time. If you do not respond by that time, they will learn to not trust you and therefore to not do business with you.

When you finally arrive at the section of the proposal with packages and cost (also review the previous chapter regarding packages), explain the packages in this manner:

> *"Package #1 is exactly what you asked for and comes in under your stated budget. You expressed these needs, and the package will take care of you in the near term.*
>
> *Package #2 is a slightly enhanced package to give you more variety, room for growth, and to accommodate more departments. Your most desired items on your wish list were incorporated into this package.*
>
> *Finally, Package #3 incorporates the best of all worlds. I included it so you will know what is possible down the road. However, if you want it today this is what you will receive."*

Draw a picture in words of exactly what it is they can expect and powerful reasons why they should take this last package under serious consideration.

Make certain everyone understands and is in agreement with your stated justifications. You are now firming up the credibility and trust you have been building ever since your first contact.

Nice Girl Sales Tips

1. Give a copy of your proposal to each person in attendance.
2. Immediately ask: *"Has anything changed since we last met?"*
3. Answer only the specific questions that are posed.
4. Do not add any additional information.
5. Once everyone agrees there are no additional questions,

ask your audience the following: *"Are you ready to proceed?"*

6. Outline your agenda and then proceed as stated.

7. Read your proposal line by line.

8. Scan the audience for body language and facial expressions.

9. Stop and address any unusual gesture or expression.

10. After each section ask for questions.

11. Address only the question asked.

12. Take notes if you do not know the answer.

13. Promise a doable timeline to get the answer and keep your promise.

14. If no questions arise, proceed to the package page.

15. State: *"I have outlined three packages for your consideration, incorporating all of the information you shared. It does not matter to me which package you choose. I just want to do the very best possible for your company. Each of these packages will address your needs and your wish list is addressed in packages two and three."*

16. Read through each package.

17. Again, look for facial expressions and body language.

18. As you finish reading each package, give a one-minute explanation of why and how you put it together.

19. Ask for questions after describing each package, and answer accordingly.

21

Conclude the Sale, or, How to Close Naturally

I promised to teach you an easy, natural close. Now is the time to deliver on that promise.

Think back to all of the preparation you have done. You met with the prospect once, twice, or several times. Due to your proficiency of relationship-building skills, your prospect has confided in you her innermost thoughts, wishes, and desires. You took careful notes in your prospect's words and translated it all into a factual proposal. You are delivering everything your prospect wants and needs. Typically, most salesmen will not go to all this effort for a sale. Your competition is dust. You elevated yourself to partner by helping your prospect achieve her goals. Once her goals are achieved, she will look good and you will be the one who helped her get there. The favor you showed her will not be forgotten.

Your prospect's words led you to write a thoughtful proposal with not one but three acceptable packages. The only possible question left to ask your prospect and soon-to-be client is:

"Which package do you prefer?"

That's it! Isn't that easy? You concluded a conversation, followed up by:

> *"Which package can I get for you?"*

The Most Difficult Part of the Sale

Do you remember I told you to practice smiling the night before? There is a saying, "He or she who speaks first, loses."

Once you ask the question, you MUST sit back confidently (knowing full well you did an outstanding job), smile, and wait.

Even if there is fifteen minutes of silence, You *must* sit quietly and smile confidently.

Eventually the client will recognize the ball is in their court and they need to respond. The client might say:

> *"I want Package #2."*

Or the client will ask you a question. Again, only answer that specific question. Do not offer additional information. If you do not understand the question, or if it throws you off course, ask:

> *"Why?"* or *"Would you please explain?"*

Your heart may be pounding so fast you aren't able to think clearly. One of those questions will work in your favor to gain a little extra time and composure. Collect your thoughts, and answer intelligently by focusing on the issue.

After you answer, there may be no real response from your prospect/client. You may take it one step further and continue the conversation by asking:

> *"Did I answer your question?"*

Followed by:

> *"Do you have any other questions?"*

At this point, the client is still thinking about what to do next. By not talking, you put the pressure on the client to make the next move.

Assuming everything was executed to plan, and you came this far, most likely you will receive a:

> *"Yes, that is satisfactory."*

If the client slowly and hesitantly picks up the conversation, you may again ask about preference:

> *"Are you leaning toward one package versus another? I would be happy to give my opinion. Obviously #3 will be the most profitable for me, but it may not be right for you at this time. I just wanted you to know everything we are capable of providing."*
>
> *"If you are wavering between #1 and #2, this is why I would pick Package #2 (give the merits for this package) if I were in your position."*

Make your explanation short and to the point. Note you will only offer your suggestion if the client is having a difficult time choosing. Otherwise, remain silent and smile. Most often, clients know what they need and do not want to be told.

By now, the new client will have picked a package to their liking. The next-to-last closing question may have to do with delivery.

> *"When can I expect to take delivery on Package #2?"*
> *"We can have Package #2 installed by December 1. Will this date fit your timetable?"*

Once you have agreement on the changeover date, you know you almost have the sale.

The Sale Is Not Official Until...
- You have the sale authorized with signature
- Changeover takes place without difficulty
- You remain in touch every step of the way
- Buyer's remorse period has passed

After my very first sale, fifteen years ago, I wound up with my having to shred the new client's deposit check and the contract. Buyer's remorse had set in within twenty-four hours.

Brand-new to sales, I most likely did not provide enough assurance that my client's satisfaction with the changeover would be met.

Back to the finishing process—you still have some work ahead of you. One more time, explain in detail how your client will take delivery of what you are offering, including the timeline for each step to take place. Very likely your client was not listening the first time as they were concentrating on making a decision.

And the Final Closing Actions Are...
• Turn to the contract page for signature.
• Hand the client one of your attractive pens.
• State the following: *"All I need is your authorization here."*
   NOTE: Do not say:

> *"Sign here."*
> or
> *"I need your signature here."*

Any variation of the word "sign" makes people believe they are signing away their life. Instead, it is best to use the word "authorize."

Use these words:
"Please authorize the contract here."

In this phase, you are still relationship building utilizing the Nice Girl methodology. The word "authorize" indicates that the client has power. For added impact, hand a nice-looking pen to the person about to authorize the contract.

When you are giving directions on where to authorize, make certain the proper line is highlighted in yellow and marked with a big "X." Anything you can do to make authorizing a contract easy for your client will speed up the process and put you in a more favorable light.

There is one other possible statement you need to make after asking for authorization. This extra statement is purely dependent upon how your business is conducted:

> *"And all we need to get you started in the process is a deposit for $75,000."*

Whether you ask for a deposit or not, at this point you will need to sit back, once again, with a big smile on your face and wait silently.

As the client moves the contract back toward you, offer the pen to be kept as a token of your appreciation. Give a sincere *"Thank you"* to your new client. This would be the appropriate time to reassure your client that an excellent choice was made, and that you will do everything possible to insure a smooth transition.

Before you leave, ask your client if she prefers you make a copy of the contract for her right then or if she prefers you send her a copy. Proceed accordingly as the Nice Girl would do.

Once you are ready to leave the meeting, shake hands with everyone in the room while looking them in the eye, and thank each person profusely.

Once again, tell the person who authorized the paperwork that you will remain in touch throughout the process. Give assurances that you will remain on top of the process throughout the changeover.

Explain the next two steps that you will be taking, and when they can expect to hear from you next.

As soon as you reach your office, complete two tasks immediately:

1. Hand the contract in for processing
2. Write a thank-you note to everyone who attended the authorization meeting.

Do everything in your power to make the transition smooth and fun for everyone. If hardware or software is being installed, make arrangements to be there part of the time. Bring bagels, muffins, or doughnuts with you.

Make certain to introduce employees to people on your staff so that everyone feels comfortable with the changeover.

No matter what happens on your end in terms of problems, do not communicate them to your new client. Make the transition as seamless as possible. Always smile and look happy.

If your profit on the sale is large enough, offer to take your new client to lunch. Meeting for lunch is a great way to become comfortable with your client on a personal level. You may also wish to invite the other people who helped influence the decision. If it is a smaller-scale sale, bring a box of candy to the office. Clients appreciate the gesture and the thoughtfulness. Even if they cannot go to lunch with you, they will remember your kind offer. A thank-you gift of any caliber will be appreciated and remembered.

As long as you take excellent care of this client from the moment they authorize the contract, you will be well on your way to developing repeat business and referrals. Most importantly, you are becoming proficient at building relationships and implementing the Nice Girl philosophy.

After all is said and done, you may receive a thank-you note for the excellent service you provided. Collect these notes and/or emails for your portfolio. The next time someone asks you, *"How do I know you are any good?"* you will be able to pull out your collection of testimonials to prove the point.

Nice Girl Sales Tips

1. Mentally review everything you have done up until this point and feel confident.
2. Simply ask (with a big smile), *"Which package do you prefer?"*
3. Remain silent until someone else speaks first.
4. Keep smiling!
5. Answer only specific questions.
6. Ask if the answer resolved the question.
7. Ask for additional questions.
8. Move to the next closing statement: *"All I need is your authorization here."*
9. Offer a nice pen to be used for the authorization and later, as a keepsake.
10. If required, state *"All I need is a deposit for $75,000."*
11. Explain the steps for taking delivery of the services and a timeline for each step.
12. Give assurances of a wise choice and smooth transition.
13. Offer a choice of making a copy of the contract there or sending an official copy later.
14. Thank everyone profusely and shake hands with everyone in the authorization meeting.
15. When you're back at the office, process the contract immediately.

16. Write thank-you notes to everyone who helped influence the decision.
17. Stay on top of every detail for delivery, and communicate positive details to the client.
18. Do your best to resolve all issues from your end without revealing the details to the client.
19. Depending upon the nature and size of the sale, bring in food or offer to go out for lunch.
20. As other members of your team need to visit the account, make personal introductions.
21. Develop goodwill between your company and the client company.

22
Build Repeat Business and Referrals

When you are hunting for prospects, you have to work hard to obtain their interest. After a sale, you will have to work at least twice as hard to keep the clients satisfied and up-to-date with news of your company.

There are several Nice Girl strategies to help resolve the time commitment of staying in touch with everyone, yet enable you to sell more. The first step is to keep your database management system handy and up-to-date. Bring the calendar up every day and keep it up all day long. By inputting all contacts, tasks, and notes, you will be on top of your sales game. The most important result is that your efficiency will greatly increase.

As you review your to-do list and contact your prospects and clients, let them know about any new development within your company. Clients like to know that your company is aspiring to grow as well.

When you do call or visit, try to find out what their new developments might be. The easiest and least expensive prospect to convert is your current client. An accountant shared that it costs six times as much to acquire a new client than it does to develop additional business with the current client.

Always be aware if there are further opportunities within the account. Keep in constant contact with your client and over time, meet as many people within the client's company as possible.

As you read about the client's industry and/or company, ask yourself how the news is affecting them. Will it have any bearing on your current services and future services you were hoping to sell them? Let the client know you are aware of the issues and ask his or her opinion.

If you see a complimentary article or hear an interview about the company or your contact, let them know. Call or write to congratulate them on the good press. Anything you can do to let your clients know you have their interest in mind will go a long way in building trusted relationships and future business.

Many salesmen run after making a sale. They prefer to make the quick hit sales, believing that account management is too time-consuming. Once everything is in place, the new client will never see or hear from the salesman again.

On the other hand, the Nice Girl will first ask for a report card on how her company is performing, to judge if they have lived up to promises, and to straighten out any unforeseen problems. Next she will alternate her monthly contact by phone, email, mailer, handwritten note, and in-person visits. On a quarterly basis, she may send out an email greeting card for good cheer. Be assured, the Nice Girl gets the sale!

We spoke about strategic selling earlier. However, if you were only able to begin the sales process with one department, slowly but surely begin inquiring about the other departments.

Ask if the rest of the company will benefit from the service you are providing the one department. If the answer is "yes," ask if you might be introduced to the other department heads. If your service is top-notch all the way, you will slowly win over the rest of the company.

Now that the switchover to your service has been made and you have happy clients, ask for referrals. Do they have associates at other companies who might make use of the same services? Do they belong to organizations to which they might refer you? Do they know others in the same jobs as they have?

A referral already has the knowledge that you provide an excellent service. It will be a much easier sell and a shorter sales cycle.

Once you are introduced to another prospect, reward the person making the introduction. Write a thank-you note, and take them to lunch. Make certain the reward fits your budget and the personality of the recipient.

If someone offers help in a way that you had not anticipated, such as speaking in front of a group—go for it! Try something new and see what happens. The new avenue may very well expand your horizons and enable you to sell more than you ever anticipated.

Nice Girl Sales Tips

1. Use a contact management system that will work easily for you.
2. Contact your clients monthly and vary the methods.

3. Look for news regarding your clients' companies.

4. Maintain an open dialogue about each other's company.

5. Build relationships within each company.

6. Develop opportunity for repeat business.

7. Ask for referrals.

8. Accumulate thank-you notes and emails for your portfolio.

9. Accept the offered helping hand.

Goal-Setting

Keep re-evaluating your goals. Think about what you want to accomplish next, what it will take, and how to go about executing the plan. You may need to revisit the idea of finding a mentor or a business coach.

Most certainly you will want to educate yourself on related subject matter and on new topics. The better versed you are, the more successful you will become.

At some point, you may wish to begin a business of your own. Entrepreneurship for women has become a rewarding, new culture in American society. A popular buzzword phrase for entrepreneurs today is "multiple streams of income." This is an updated way of saying: "diversify." Traditionally, diversification was only for big business, but today entrepreneurs can do the same. The Nice Girl entrepreneur can now devise many new avenues for making money. A common solution is to package similar information in the form of lectures, CDs, e-books, reports, articles, workshops, and licensing. Once you find what your prospects and clients want, it is up to you to deliver. Keep an open mind and listen to those requests. You will find new paths unimagined before. Women have begun to succeed in bigger numbers building their own multimillion-dollar businesses.

Getting back to traditional sales, look into channel sales to determine if that is applicable for what you sell. For instance, shoe manufacturers distribute both through retail and wholesale stores in order to sell more shoes and to develop their brand name.

The point is to begin thinking creatively about what you sell and about how you may more easily expand your territory or audience. By tackling different avenues, you may find a new stream of income.

While sales may entail long hours when you first get started, it will become fun and rewarding over time. If you enjoy what you are selling and believe in it, do not give up. Keep at it every day. The sales will come.

And as you are working your plan every day, keep an updated list of short-term and long-term goals. It feels good to cross off the completed goals and presents a healthy challenge to add new goals to the list, all the while keeping your eye on the long-term goals.

Your list should recognize both company and personal goals. Tell yourself how much you will sell each month. If you have a quota, determine what the percentage of attainment will be.

If you are at a company that has quarterly and yearly bonuses, challenge yourself to meet those goals. Include additional bonuses, such as gift checks and trips as they are awarded throughout the year.

Write down all of the possible goals that are achievable for you now and ones that are slightly above your head. An amazing thing happens when you promise yourself that you will do your best to achieve these goals—you will actually find yourself achieving them! You will find it very exciting to participate in this process.

If you work for a smaller company or are in business for yourself, challenge yourself to achieve higher sales amounts each month. Add that challenge to the goal of achieving higher profit margins each succeeding month. And finally, each month add one or two more new clients than you had in the previous month.

You will feel a great deal of satisfaction looking back on the six-month mark, and at the end of the year, seeing just how far you have come. Tracking yourself for higher closing percentages, more clients, and higher profits becomes thrilling because you accomplished everything on your own.

Another idea is to challenge yourself to get into a well-known company that previously you thought impossible to crack. Figure out creative ways to get to the decision maker.

Achieving the challenges you set for yourself will add to your self-confidence and poise. New prospects will recognize that you are successful and will be eager to do business with you. Your hard work will all add up to a heftier income.

Now that you are about to achieve a larger income, you need to set personal goals for yourself. What do you like to do in your spare time? If travel is one of your pleasures, plan an affordable trip for when you hit your targets. Do you prefer fine dining? Plan where you will dine with your favorite companion when you achieve the next sale.

Nice Girl Sales Tips

1. Work your plan every day.
2. Set short-term and long-term goals.
3. Set company sales goals as well as personal goals.
4. Re-evaluate your goals monthly and always set a few goals that are just beyond your experience.
5. Write your goals down and read them out loud.
6. Every six months, look back to see what you have achieved, and revise your list.
7. Reward yourself for achieving goals, as appropriate.

23
Words of Wisdom from Multimillionaire Entrepreneurs

Here are words of wisdom from women who have become highly successful in their own right. Their words are listed in the form of sales tips. I enjoy and relate to these quotes and wish to pass them on to you:

Nice Girl Sales Tips

1. Get rid of the F word—fear.
2. Think of duties as, *"What do I **get** to do today?"* rather than, *"What do I **have** to do today?"*
3. Sell what you are passionate about.
4. Stay focused.
5. The difference between a successful entrepreneur and one who failed is the successful entrepreneur never gave up.
6. Give back to your community.
7. Do philanthropic work.
8. Remember, no one decision sinks a company but procrastination will.
9. Plan quiet time to think about your business.
10. Think B-I-G.
11. Listen to your intuition.

12. There is a good reason why the rearview mirror is so tiny and the windshield is so large. It's good to remember where you came from but don't dwell on it—keep pushing forward!

Final Remarks

In its final form, the Nice Girl sales personality is driven by goal setting, relationship building, solution-based selling, goal achievement, and recognition that the final sale was a win-win for all concerned. It also encompasses rewarding yourself for having done an outstanding job. There were times when I was having so much fun, it was hard to believe that I was being paid to sell. I wish the same for you, and all the success you dream of!

My last piece of advice is to play each game to the end. Even though you think it will be a long shot to earn the business, keep going because often there are "happily ever after" endings.

I hope you have found useful information in this book. For additional sales help, visit http://www.smoothsale.net.

You will find sales advice in various forms:

Free of Charge
- The bimonthly *Sales Tips* e-zine is distributed by email and is permission based.
- Frequently recorded audio sales tips on the Smooth Sale website.
- Tune in to the online and syndicated radio show, "Smooth Sale Strategies for Success" on www.womensradio.com.

Fee-Based Services

- Sales training for your team on your premises tailored to your company.
- On-site workshops for 8+ designed for your group.
- Smooth Sale Tele-Cruise seminar for groups of 8+ ("Cruise to Your Success!"). No destination is too far with training by telephone scheduled for your group at your convenience.
- Licensing of sales training materials. This train-the-leaders program includes training for you to teach your teams and delivers ongoing support.
- Speaking engagements for conferences and training seminars.

Products

The Smooth Selling four-hour, four-CD audio seminar for a comprehensive study to improve your selling skills (comprised of four, sixty-minute CDs) walks you through the entire sales cycle, teaching you how to begin as a trusted consultant, transfer midway to partner status to secure business, and finally, harvest repeat business, referrals, and testimonials. The set makes a perfect gift for your auto university.

Special Reports

Many new topics covering additional sales skills and strategies for building a better business presented in report style and on CD are coming! The most often requested is "Specific Questions to Ask at Each Stage of the Sales Cycle." Included will be the order of questions to ask at each stage and the significance of each. These questions will greatly strengthen your positioning and selling skills.

Please email sales@smoothsale.net for sales questions or feedback, or call our local number at 415-615-6887 or our toll free number 1-800-704-1499.

Wishing you,

Enjoyment in your endeavors, Nice Girl success, and a Smooth Sale!

Elinor Stutz

Appendix: Resources

Below is a listing of resources as they appear on my website http://www.smoothsale.net/resources.shtml:

- http://www.wbenc.org
  Certification as a minority- and woman-owned business.
- http://www.ewomennetwork.com
  Effective power networking among women, with branches of the organization across the U.S. and Canada.
- http://www.ewomenpublishingnetwork.com
  For authors in any stage of the process seeking help and guidance to ensure success.
- http://www.womenscalendar.org
  List of events for women across the U.S.
- http://www.womensradio.com
  Read helpful business news tips and articles, even start your own radio show.
- http://smoothsale.audioacrobat.com/
  Put live voice on your website or in your email with ease. Try it free for thirty days.
- http://www.womenscommunity.com
  An online global networking and mentoring community for women.
- http://www.wealthybaglady.com
  A mentoring company designed for businesswomen.

- http://www.nawbo.org
  National Association of Women Business Owners—chapters across the country.
- http://www.verizon.com
  Find any business or person within the U.S.
- http://www.superpages.com
  Business lookup by several methods including reverse directory and phone numbers.
- http://www.hoovers.com
  Mostly fee-based providing detailed information about most known companies.
- http://www.contractingrg.com
  Learn how to become a contractor for the government and reap the benefits.
- http://dmoz.org/
  Web directory of Internet resources.
- http://www.fita.org/
  Federation of International Trade Associations—lists of sites to grow your business.

Index

W

About the Author

Photo by: Jeanne de Polo

Elinor Stutz, founder and CEO of Smooth Sale, specializes in sales training for entrepreneurs, network marketers, and beginning salespeople. After eleven years of working in corporate sales, Elinor now reveals her self-taught approach to sales that leveraged her success beyond that of her most seasoned colleagues.

Beginning her career as a copier saleswoman with a phone book as her only source of leads, Elinor was able to rise past the chauvinism in her male-dominated office and turn ice cold leads into trusted partners. She went on to become the top salesperson in her region. As she advanced her career with other opportunities in networked printers and high tech, recognition in the form of Presidents' Clubs and Regional and National Awards accompanied every step.

Elinor's past client roster includes Visa, Sony, Hewlett-Packard, and U.S. Geological Survey, as well as a growing number of high-tech companies in Silicon Valley. Committed to passing on her knowledge to others, Elinor emphasizes relationship building and adapting sales techniques to suit individual personalities. As an author, instructor, public speaker, and radio guest and show host, she has helped countless individuals and companies incorporate this practice into their businesses.

With the aid of her many services and products including books, CDs, articles, and a sales tips e-zine, Elinor has taught business people across the country to overcome their fears and obstacles of selling through the art of the Smooth Sale.